WHEN WE WERE YOUNG

Memories of Childhood

When We Were Young

Memories of Childhood

A GRAHAM TARRANT BOOK

DAVID & CHARLES

Newton Abbot   London   North Pomfret (Vt)

This anthology copyright © NSPCC 1987
Copyright for each item: the author or author's agents
Photograph of Keith Waterhouse by Henry Grant

British Library Cataloguing in Publication Data
When we were young: memories of childhood.
—— (A Graham Tarrant book).
1. Biography
920'.02   CT105
ISBN 0-7153-8995-5

Designed by Grub Street Design, London

Phototypeset by AKM Associates (UK) Ltd.
Ajmal House, Hayes Road, Southall, London
and printed in Great Britain by
Butler & Tanner Ltd, Frome and London
for David & Charles Publishers plc
Brunel House Newton Abbot Devon

Published in the United States of America
by David & Charles Inc
North Pomfret Vermont 05053 USA

ACKNOWLEDGEMENTS

The NSPCC gratefully acknowledges the generous contribution of the authors who together have made this book possible.

The NSPCC and the publishers gratefully acknowledge permission to quote from the following works:
Not the Whole Truth by Patrick Lichfield, published by Constable; *Heyhoe!* by Rachael Heyhoe Flint, published by Pelham Books; *In My Wildest Dreams* by Leslie Thomas, published by Arlington Books; *Waterhouse at Large* by Keith Waterhouse, published by Michael Joseph (by permission of David Higham Associates Ltd); *Notes for a Life* by Bryan Forbes, published by William Collins Sons & Co Ltd; *Thanks to Rugby* by Bill Beaumont, published by Stanley Paul; *A Postillion Struck by Lightning* by Dirk Bogarde, published by Chatto & Windus Ltd; *Jacobs' Ladder* by David Jacobs, published by Peter Davies Ltd; *Amiscellany*: My Life, My Music by John Amis, published by Faber & Faber Ltd; *Jolly Super* by Jilly Cooper, published by Methuen London; *A Yorkshire Boyhood* by Roy Hattersley, published by Chatto & Windus Ltd; *A Backdoor to Heaven* by Lionel Blue, published and copyright 1979 by Darton, Longman & Todd Ltd; *The Small World of Fred Hoyle* by Sir Fred Hoyle, published by Michael Joseph; extract from the feature 'Duke of Westminster' by kind permission of the Sunday Express Magazine; *My Family and Other Animals* by Gerald Durrell, published by Allen & Unwin.

CONTENTS

CHILDREN'S PARTY

HRH THE PRINCESS MARGARET, COUNTESS OF SNOWDON

WHEN I WAS a little girl, five or six maybe, we had to go to children's parties. This was before the last war. These we dreaded – mostly because there was usually a conjuror – experts we distrusted.

'Would the little girl in the pink dress in the front row please come up here and help me', they'd say with a smile that made it quite clear that one was going to be made a fool of. It happened too often.

Once, at one of these affairs, dressed in my frilly dress, I placed myself firmly in the fifth row and refused to be moved. I sat with head bowed throughout the entertainment, praying to the Good Lord that the conjuror wouldn't ask me to help him.

He didn't.

That childish experience gave me confidence in the power of prayer, which I've believed in ever since.

Margaret

What I Did On My Holidays

FRANK MUIR

I T WAS THE perfect holiday. I remember packing my suitcase with tremendous care, emptying it out and beginning again until everything lay in neat and unruffled order. I was travelling alone so I planned the journey carefully and rehearsed it endlessly in my mind. When the day came I bade farewell to my loved ones and set off. I had four days of bliss and returned home, safely with my memories. I was aged six, and I had gone to my grandmother's house, four doors down the road.

I did not go away on holiday again until I was grown-up. As I lived at the seaside there was nowhere better to go away *to*. I was once taken into the countryside for a day and I was appalled. We lived at Broadstairs and I sang in the choir at the parish church. Or, to be more accurate, I turned up but did not actually give voice. The lure of the choir was the five shillings a quarter that the job paid. My only hope of hanging on to this bonanza was to conceal from the authorities the fact that I could not sing (a fact only too clear to Radio 4 listeners) and so I developed a technique of lurking in the background at all times and, during hymns, miming.

Another bonus to being a songster was the Annual Choir Outing. The vicar laid on a horse-brake. This was an ancient Edwardian vehicle which had plied between Ramsgate and Pegwell Bay until it became so unroadworthy that no horse could be persuaded to pull it. We all sat on plank seats facing each other, I and two other voiceless delinquents on the uncovered top deck, and proceeded in a light, warm, summer drizzle towards the Kent village of Pluck's Gutter (what magic names these old hamlets have, to be sure).

We arrived at our picnic spot very late as the horse turned petulant just north of Sandwich and slowed to 1mph, but the vicar soon had us deployed in a circle on the meadow grass, clutching our brawn sandwiches. 'We are now,' he announced with a ring in his voice, 'in the midst of Nature!'

In which case, was the choristers' unspoken thought, the sooner this holiday is over and we get back to smelly seaweed and damp sand the better.

If your bottom is uncomfortable on sand you merely have to wiggle a bit and the sand conforms to your shape. Nature does not do this. You sit on a tussock and what happens? A sharp piece of long grass goes up the leg of your shorts causing brief agony, you are tilted sideways causing you to drop your brawn sandwich into a small

but active community of black beetles, and the suspiciously warm patch on which you are now sitting is a reminder that this is a pasture on which sheep have safely grazed.

Nature, of which there is a considerable quantity in the countryside, is full of fauna, as well as prickly flora which scratches your ankles. The seaside has little bits of fauna but these are mostly harmless and frequently edible, eg shrimps. Insect life at the seaside is benign, mostly a few little hopping things in the sand. Nature, on the other hand, offers whole regiments of malevolent predators whose tiny little teeth do damage far in excess of the beast's height and fighting weight. For anybody collecting this kind of scientific data I am able to state that during forty minutes spent in a meadow adjacent to Pluck's Gutter, Kent, sitting half on a tussock and half on firmish sheep spoor, the following happened: A very large black, shiny bug, clearly in wine, flew erratically in front of me and then thudded into my forehead. A weal arose. A colony of frantic, maladjusted, and very tiny ants invaded my sandals and scurried about, biting. About two hundred thousand very small red marks arose. A cricket levitated in front of me and dropped down the front of my shirt causing me to utter a long, thin, girlish scream. A squadron of large flies with hairy legs and, by the sound of them, jet engines, strafed me and my brawn. A number of ugly lumps arose on forehead and forearms. I threw the brawn away.

So my childhood experience of holidays boiled down to two ventures: the worst, sitting on a sheep's pat at Pluck's Gutter being eaten by Nature; and the best, my four days' hols with my granny.

No holiday since has been as bad, or as good.

MY GRANDMOTHER
LADY PAMELA MOUNTBATTEN

MY GRANDMOTHER, VICTORIA, Marchioness of Milford Haven (a grand-daughter of Queen Victoria's) was the most remarkable person I have ever known. She illuminated my whole childhood and youth with a shaft of bright light which has kept her personality as strong an influence upon me now as it was at her death in 1950. To spend any length of time with her, whether for an hour or a visit of several weeks, was always a joy, either as a child or as a grown-up. She had plenty of that rare and valuable commodity in today's rushed world – time – with which she liberally endowed her visitors. She knew how to amuse a child by making a fragrant

soft ball out of cowslips, or a doll's tea set from acorns; how to put a nervous or retiring person at ease by finding out their interests; how to talk to an eminent professor or a high-ranking Service Officer on his particular subjects, about which she could often be better informed than they were. She dearly loved interesting conversation and was not averse to resounding arguments in several languages which never grew acrimonious, although they sometimes alarmed uninitiated listeners. Her knowledge was legendary; never, when she was in the house, did anyone have need of dictionary, atlas or encyclopaedia. You merely said 'Ask Grandmama', whose immediate answers were always full and fascinating. Her memory was prodigious and instantly brought history alive. What she had not lived through, she had read about voraciously.

And yet to a child she was in no way alarming because she had the gift of treating a child as an interesting person to be equally respected. I never remember wanting to be badly behaved with Grandmama; she was far too interesting and such behaviour would have been unthinkable and a waste of time. I greatly loved and admired her in every way: her courage, her philosophical and practical nature, her tremendous self-reliance, her intelligence and high standards. She was a very strong believer in the importance of family ties and support of each other, and yet she was totally independent and unpossessive herself.

There were times when my grandmother assumed more the role of a parent than grandparent to my sister and me. Coming as we did from a naval family there were long periods during the war and when my parents were stationed abroad, when they could not always have us with them. At such times our beloved grandmother would come to stay with us or we would visit her and the void would be temporarily filled.

She exerted a very strong and happy influence over our lives and personalities. This is probably why I have always believed very strongly in the importance of a good grandparent/grandchild relationship in a child's upbringing. I can only hope that now I find myself in the happy role of being a grandmother, I shall be able in some small degree to continue this tradition of a special relationship with my own grandchildren.

JOSS SPIVVIS

ROALD DAHL

ONE OF MY most enduring memories of early childhood was my friendship with Joss Spivvis!

It all started in the early nineteen-twenties, not long after my father and my eldest sister had both died within a few weeks of one another. The remainder of our large family, consisting of my mother and six children, had moved to a house in Llandaff, near Cardiff, which was called Cumberland Lodge.

The gardener that my mother engaged to look after everything outdoors was a short, broad-shouldered, middle-aged Welshman with a pale brown moustache whose name was Jones. But to us children he very soon became known as Joss Spivvis, or more often simply Joss. And very rapidly Joss became a friend to us all, to my brother and me and my four sisters. Everyone loved him, but I loved him most of all. I adored him. I worshipped him, and whenever I was not at school, I used to follow him around and watch him at his work and listen to him talk.

I was seven years old at the time and I was already a day-boy at Llandaff Cathedral School where, as I remember very clearly, I had to stay on for an additional forty minutes every afternoon for extra lessons in reading because I was so backward. But each day, when I escaped from the classroom at last, I would run all the way home so that I could have half an hour with Joss in the garden before it was time for him to get on his bicycle and ride back to his wife.

The holidays were best because then I could spend all day with him, and by all day I mean literally the whole of the day, lunchtime included. And endless were the stories he told me as I stood close to him while he dug the kitchen garden or weeded the flowerbeds, and if it was raining we would be in the potting shed or in the greenhouse or in the harness room. I liked it best of all when he told me about his own boyhood in the Rhondda Valley, when he was sent down the coalmines at the age of eleven. He had the Welshman's love of speech and song, and when he was describing something to me, his flowery sentences would hold me enthralled.

'Five o'clock every morning six days a week we reported for work at the pithead,' he said, 'and me just a skinny little nipper wearing my grandad's worn-out old jacket as an overcoat, and I was always shivering shivering shivering. You don't half shiver at five in the morning when you're young and skinny. Then into the cage we all went and when they let go the winding-gear, we all dropped like a stone into the black black hole for miles and miles, and it fell so fast your feet left the floor and your stomach came up to your throat, and every time I went down I thought the cable had broken and we were going to go right on falling until we came to the very

centre of the earth where everything was white-hot boiling lava.'

'Did it ever crash, Joss, that cage?'

'Lots of 'em crashed,' he said. 'But never with me in it or I wouldn't be here.'

'You mean the wire broke?'

'Not the wire,' he said, 'It was the brakes on the winding-gear that went wrong. And then the cage would go shooting downwards faster and faster for thousands of feet until it smashed into the bottom of the shaft and all the men inside would be turned into strawberry jam.'

'What did you do, Joss, down there in the coalmine? Did you help to get the coal out?'

'My job was to help with the pit ponies,' Joss said, 'to get them out of their stalls and harness them up to the trolleys and then lead them to the coalface. Poor little blind beggars they were too, that never saw the light of day, but they were all my friends. The foreman on each coalface carried a canary with him in a titchy little cage and the cage would be hung from the roof of the tunnel near where the men were working on the face.'

'A canary? Why a canary, Joss?'

'To tell us if there were poisonous gases in the tunnel. A bird will die much quicker than a man if there's any gas around, so as long as the bird is chirpy and happy then everything's all right.'

'Was the canary always all right, Joss?'

'Listen to this,' he said. 'One day I was looking up and talking to the canary and at that very moment the bird toppled over and fell off its perch, stone dead. "The canary's gone over!" I shouted in my screechy high voice, because don't forget I was only eleven. "The canary's pegged it and it's lying on the floor!" I shouted, and the six men all turned and stared, and the foreman yelled, "Out! Everybody out!" But I wasn't going to leave my little pony behind to suffocate, so while all the others ran for their lives down the tunnel, I stopped and unharnessed it from the trolley and trotted it away.'

'Good for you, Joss. That was a jolly brave thing to do.'

'*You* wouldn't have left it behind either, would you?'

'I hope I wouldn't. But I'd have been awfully frightened.'

'Oh, I was frightened all right. Coalmines was horrible places in those days, my boy. Men were getting killed in them all the time.'

Endless stories about his young days Joss would tell me as I followed him round the garden. In the summer holidays my mother always took us to Norway, but during the Christmas and Easter hols I was with Joss all the time. I never ate lunch in the house with the family. I ate it with Joss in the harness room. I would perch on a sack of maize or a bale of straw while Joss sat rather grandly in an old kitchen chair that had arms on it. Then he would open his lunch-tin which had been most carefully packed by his wife that morning. The contents of the tin never varied. It contained

Roald Dahl flanked by his sisters

not only Joss's lunch but mine as well, which was provided daily as a matter of course by Mrs Jones. Thinking back on it now, I am a bit surprised that my mother allowed that good woman to buy my lunch for me six days a week without recompense, but I expect she knew what she was doing.

The lunch-tin contained four Crawford's Crackers for each of us, lightly buttered, and two large hunks of Cheddar cheese. Joss would cut his cheese into thin slices with his gardener's pruning knife, and I copied him with my own pocket-knife. And after the cheese came some of Mrs Jones's homemade cakes, either rock cakes or jam tarts. While he ate, Joss drank hot tea which he poured from a thermos. I didn't like tea so I drank nothing. And there we sat in the quiet of the harness room while Joss talked and I listened. One of his favourite subjects was the Cardiff City Football Team, and I was very quickly swept along by his enthusiasm for those heroes of the turf. Cardiff City was a fine club in those days, and if I remember rightly, it was high up in the First Division. Throughout the week, as Saturday came closer and closer,

so our excitement grew. The reason was simple. Both of us knew that we were actually going to go to the game together. We always did. Every Saturday afternoon, rain or hail or snow or sleet, Joss and I would go to Ninian Park to see the City play.

Oh, it was a great day, Saturday. Joss would work in the garden until noon, then I would emerge from the house neatly dressed in my scarlet school cap, my blazer, my flannel shorts and possibly a navy-blue overcoat, and I would hand over to him a half-crown and a shilling that my mother had given me to pay for us both.

'Don't forget to thank your mother,' he would say to me every time as he slipped the two coins into his pocket.

The shilling would pay our bus fares both ways into Cardiff, thruppence each going out, and thruppence each coming home. The half-crown, believe it or not would pay for both our entrance fees to the ground (ninepence each on the terraces), and also for our lunches. As we rode the twenty minute journey from Llandaff to Cardiff in the big red bus, our excitement began to mount, and Joss would tell me about the opposing team for that day and the star players in it who were going to threaten our heroes in Cardiff City. It might be Sheffield Wednesday or West Bromwich Albion or Manchester United or any of the fifteen others, and I would listen and remember every detail of what Joss was saying. The bus took us to within five minutes' walk of Ninian Park Football Ground, where the great matches were always played, and outside the ground we would stop at a whelk-stall that stood near the turnstiles. Joss would have a dish of jellied eels (sixpence) and I would have baked beans and two sausages on a cardboard plate (also sixpence).

Then, with an almost unbearable sense of thrill and rapture, and holding Joss tightly by the hand, I would enter the hallowed portals and we would make our way through the crowd to the highest point of the terraces, behind one of the goalposts. We had to be high up otherwise I wouldn't have seen anything.

But oh, it was thrilling to stand there among those thousands of other men cheering our heroes when they did well and groaning when they lost the ball. We knew all the players by name and to this very day, some sixty-four years later, I can still remember the names of three of them. The centre-half for Cardiff was a small bald-headed man whom Joss referred to as Little 'Ardy. His name was Hardy. One of the full-backs was Nelson. The goalkeeper was a giant called Farquharson, which my mother told me was pronounced Farkerson but which Joss pronounced Far-q-arson. Hardy, Nelson and Farquharson. Look up the records and you'll find they were there. And when Cardiff scored a goal, I would jump up and down and Joss would wave his cap in the air, shouting, 'Well played, sir! Well played!'

And after it was all over we would take the bus home again, discussing without pause the great spectacle and the famous men we had just been privileged to see.

It was always dark by the time we reached my house, and Joss, standing in the porch with his cap in his hand, would say to my mother, 'We're back safe, ma'am. We had a grand time.'

THE HEADMASTER

DEREK JAMESON

HE WORE A pince-nez, appeared to be ten feet tall and would descend like the wrath of God on small boys like myself set on making mischief. Bertram Cartwright was the name. One of the most unforgettable characters I ever met.

As Headmaster of Detmold Road Elementary Boys' School, he was like a captain without a ship. We had been rudely shifted from our redbrick Victorian monstrosity near the Hackney Marshes and these days he presided over a church hall in Bishop's Stortford. This was wartime Britain – and we were all evacuees.

His greatest pride next to 'My school,' as he would call it, was his native Staffordshire. There we were, a bunch of Cockney lads far from home, and he would regale us at Assembly with little homilies about the virtues of the Staffordshire knot, coalmining and pottery.

What tickled us most was his constant delight in leading us in the school song, written by one of the masters, to remind us that we belonged to the East End, not the rural pastures of Hertfordshire. It was over forty years ago, but I can still remember the words:

> *Detmold Road forever,*
> *It's standing firmly still;*
> *The years go past, we grow up fast,*
> *But Detmold can and will,*
> *Carry on, the burning torch,*
> *Through times both good and ill . . .*

The joke was that the Detmold we sang about with such nostalgia was anything but firm. Quite apart from the bombs falling all around it, the school was built on marshy soil and used to sink several inches every year. Workmen would come in during the summer holidays, dig huge holes under the foundations and shore up the building with fresh concrete.

With his drooping bow tie, pursed lips and tiny spectacles, Mr Cartwright naturally was the butt of our playground jokes. We called him 'Will Hay' after the screen headmaster. Since we were all crazy about the comedian, I suppose it was the Cockney way of showing respect.

'Empty tins make the most noise,' Mr Cartwright would hiss as he knocked two

heads together. Discipline was fierce in those days. Another favourite saying was 'You won't go far wrong in life if you remember what I was taught as a lad: "Eyes open, ears open, mouth shut!" '

Of course, like many another good teacher, he never practised what he preached. That endeared him to us all the more.

'Ah, I can see where you're going in life,' he would say as he tweaked the earlobe of some poor lad caught not paying attention. 'You'll end up as a lorry driver's mate.' He made it sound like a job offer from the Devil.

He never married, though rumour had it that he took a wife on his retirement not long after the war ended. Presumably he was too busy earlier running the school and playing the horses. He certainly had an eye for the ladies, as many a mother could testify.

I met Bertram Cartwright for the last time in the late forties. We walked round St Paul's Cathedral together – he was a great churchgoer – and I told him proudly that I had graduated from messenger boy to trainee reporter in Fleet Street.

'How much are they paying you?' was the first thing he wanted to know. It was a modest sum – something like £7 a week – but thinking about it makes me sad to this day.

'D'you know,' he said wistfully after a pause. 'That's more than I ever earned in a lifetime of teaching.'

He was a hard man, difficult to know and demanding only the best. But there was a magical quality about him. We sensed that he really cared about his boys. We loved him deeply.

JESUS WANTS ME FOR A SUNBEAM

BRENDA DEAN

I T IS NOT all that long ago that those with childhood illnesses were either swept off to an isolation hospital or separated very sharply from all contact with others of their age.

In my case, when scarlet fever was confirmed by the doctor, it was isolation – but very definitely at home. My mother insisted she could cope and so it was agreed

that I be confined to my own bedroom in our little Eccles house. This meant moving my brother out because, in a two-bedroomed house, we had to share a room.

Despite my mother's efforts I was pretty miserable. I couldn't even talk to my horrible little brother and he seemed to be having all the fun while I was locked away.

Then, somehow, the local Salvation Army learned of my isolation and resolved to bring a little sunshine into my life.

Each weekend of what seemed an eternity – probably about six weeks – they would come round and sing to me outside my bedroom window. I suddenly felt important: a whole band coming down our scruffy alley to sing to me. I was no longer forgotten. And they brought me a present each Sunday – usually an apple.

By the time they were halfway through their medley of songs, the neighbours too had gathered round. And they would send up messages and bits of things for me. They filled my room with sunshine. It was absolutely marvellous.

Ever since then I've had a soft spot for brass bands and particularly those of the Salvation Army. I think they do a grand job and are far too often taken for granted. It was their music and particularly 'Jesus wants me for a sunbeam' which cheered me up and convinced me that I was not totally forgotten.

I subsequently joined the local unit, as did my horrid little brother, and I was quite a dab hand at the triangle. But my singing was not up to it. I remember we would go on outings to different places on a Saturday and the day ended with a sing-song. I was so shy I had always refused to sing solo. But I was persuaded to try. For weeks I practised, but come the night . . . I stepped forward from the rest of the singing company, my red taffeta blouse and tie neatly in place, my black skirt brushed down, and opened my mouth for the solo – and nothing came out. There I was, in the spotlight, surrounded by people but oh, so lonely on that stage. I was terrified and my shyness completely overcame me. Then suddenly the song I was to sing was being sung: my friends in the Company had come in behind me in support and I felt such a warm glow of love around me. My shyness drifted away and before the song was over, there I was singing with them.

But my real chance to say 'thank you' to the Salvation Army came recently, when I was asked to address the officer cadets in training at their college at Sunbury on Thames. It meant quite an upheaval of my diary to get there and I'm sure my staff thought I had suddenly lost sight of my priorities. I hadn't – and I enjoyed the afternoon's discussion tremendously. I felt, if anything, considerably recharged.

And not least when the officer cadets all stood up to give me a special rendering of 'Jesus wants me for a sunbeam' – why, with my new found confidence, all shyness gone, I could have even led them in the singing!

HARROW IN THE FRAME

PATRICK LICHFIELD

AS THE TIME for me to enter Harrow grew steadily closer, my prep school masters grew steadily more embarrassed by the indecorous illustrations of couples on sofas that began to decorate the margins of my homework. Developed by a schoolmaster uncle of mine, holiday-cramming me for the Common Entrance exam, they were designed to illustrate the difference between the Active and the Passive Mode, a distinction which I cared little about at the time but would have great cause to remember in years to come.

This academic preparation, rigorous as it was, paled into utter insignificance beside my grandfather's determined efforts to instil in me what he considered to be an essential working knowledge of the Lore and Legend of Harrow, a hefty but unwritten tome that had been steadily accumulating since John Lyon first endowed the school in 1571. Harrow, it seemed, was strong on Tradition, not least in the vexed matter of the school uniform, a complex and time-honoured dress code that signalled one's precise position on the ladder of achievement by awarding, or withholding, rights (or 'privs') to variously coloured scarves, ties and handkerchiefs.

A coloured ribbon on a straw hat, a button fastened here or unfastened there could, apparently, make all the difference; I struggled through endless summer evenings inserting and removing collar-studs and cuff-links until my fingertips ached and my mind reeled. My least favourite item of all was the inaptly named Eton collar, a stiff, white, starched affair that extended itself half way across the shoulders and which all young boys were expected to wear until they reached the regulation height of 5'2" and moved on to the equally traditional, and equally uncomfortable, tail-coat and long grey trousers. If (or so far as my grandfather was concerned when) I became a member of a First Eleven or First Fifteen, I would be invited to assume the ultimate 'Blood's Priv', the distinctive grey waistcoat of 'The Phil', an élite within an élite that had long since abandoned its early interest in philately to become a self-perpetuating mutual admiration society for sporty scholars.

I never made it into 'The Phil'; I had more than enough trouble making it into long trousers. My height when I entered Harrow was 4'10" and it remained so, stubbornly, for at least another two and a half years; my early adolescence was spent striving to grow taller whilst above me a race of supermen, several yards high with broken voices, effortlessly negotiated the labyrinthine subtleties of what I began to realise was not so much an independent school as an independent culture.

I read recently of a new housemaster at Harrow being shown around his quarters by the Head of House, a surprisingly short tour which ended at a green baize door.

'Everything that happens on this side of the door is your responsibility,' said the boy. 'Everything beyond it is mine. When you wish to enter my side of the House you will knock and wait to be invited.'

I'd be tempted to dismiss this story as pure apocrypha were it not that in my House just such a door existed, marking off the housemaster's 'Private Side' where new boys spent their first term in protective custody before being thrust, untimely, into the hothouse world beyond.

Once through that door, it was every boy for himself, and the weakest to the wall. I dreaded it, particularly on the last day of the holidays when the determination not to blub was at its weakest. I even ran away once, realising too late that the real trick is to have something to run to, rather than from. I, having no clear goals, simply hung around London's parks and Underground stations for a day and a half waiting to be discovered by the police to whom I duly unfolded a lengthy and highly polished story about a man who'd invited me home to look at his stamp collection. My return to school was further delayed by a day spent happily travelling around London in a police car consistently just failing to identify my abductor and I rounded things off with a virtuoso imitation of acute appendicitis, a desperate ploy that resulted only in the speedy removal of one very small, very healthy appendix.

One of Harrow's more genteel customs was that boys in their last term distributed photographs of themselves to a select list of those who were left behind. As these tokens of a life beyond the walls spread all too slowly around my room, I realised that my relatively unique position as one of only four or five camera-owners in the school could be converted into sorely needed hard cash. Further research revealed that the photographs were taken by Hill and Saunders who used a huge and extremely formal plate camera at half a crown a shot. I, using my extremely informal Kodak Retinette, did it for ninepence.

The money, when added to the savings made by not putting stamps on my infrequent letters to my father, allowed me to extend my equipment to include an exposure meter and a tiny flash gun; my room gained, as an added decorative motif, a crunching carpet of used blue bulbs as I transferred my photographic allegiance from cows to stopped-action ping-pong balls. My camera accompanied me everywhere, particularly to sports fixtures, where I took great delight in capturing the McCorquodale brothers' discomfiture as their mother spoon fed them with Royal Jelly. And when I discovered that every film handed over every counter of every Boots the Chemist came straight to Harrow for processing, I swiftly made some new friends and spent hours processing prints in West Street.

The school play, *King Lear*, provided further photographic opportunities, although my experiments with ping-pong balls proved sadly inadequate to the task of freezing the flight of Gloucester's plucked-out eyeballs, a pair of peeled grapes that hit the stage with a stomach-turning squish. Gruesome props such as these were the hallmarks of my House Master, Ronald Watkins, a Shakespearian scholar with an

international reputation who always directed the school play and always managed a first-night smile when presented with a signed copy of the latest Barbara Cartland opus.

A year later when, despite endless rehearsals in the privacy of my room, I failed to capture Hollywood interest for my cameo role as Third, or possibly Fourth, Roman Citizen (sole line as I recall: 'Burn, burn, burn') I decided to be a Test match cricketer rather than a film star and cajoled my way into the under-sixteen team chosen to play Eton away. At the tea-interval, hearing that the Queen was there inspecting the cadet force, I rushed off to take what would have been my first Royal pictures, had an officious cadet not ripped the film from my camera.

from Not the Whole Truth

CONVERSATION WITH MY FATHER

MAX HASTINGS

NOTHING I CAN say about my own memories of childhood can match the wit and charm of the piece my father, Macdonald Hastings, wrote in the early nineteen-fifties, for the magazine he then edited, *Country Fair*. I am ashamed to say that it perfectly captures the flavour, if not the full enormity of my childhood misdeeds.

· CONVERSATION WITH MY SON ·
[The scene is the garden of our cottage on the Berkshire Downs]

'*Can I have some nails for my hammer, Daddy?*'
'It isn't *your* hammer; it's mine. And what do you intend doing with the nails?'
'*I'm making a soap-box car.*'
'Where?'
'*Up at the toolshed. It's quite all right, Daddy. I'm not doing any damage to your things. Really I'm not.*'
'What's that stuff on your hands?'
'*Just paint.*'
'Just paint? You've got some on your face, too. No, don't rub it off on your sleeve. Haven't you got a handkerchief?'

'It's in my other trousers.'

'But surely you've got more than one handkerchief? Here, use mine.'

'Thanks, Daddy.'

'Now, where did you get this paint?'

'It isn't any good to anybody, really, Daddy.'

'I didn't ask you whether it was any good. I asked you where you found it.'

'Somebody had thrown it away with the junk in the toolshed.'

'What led you to suppose that somebody had thrown it away?'

'The tin was jolly rusty.'

What have you been doing with it?'

'Just painting.'

'That's self-evident. I want to know what you've been painting.'

'The kiddie-car.'

'Clare's kiddie-car?'

'I asked her if she'd like it in another colour and she said she would.'

'So you did it to oblige your little sister? Where is she now?'

'Up at the toolshed.'

'What's she doing?'

'Riding the kiddie-car.'

'The one you've just painted?'

'I told her it was wet paint; but she wouldn't wait, Daddy.'

'Just you wait till your mother hears about this. I thought you two seemed suspiciously quiet this morning.'

The young
Max Hastings
exercising his
critical faculties

'Where are you going, Daddy?'

'Where do you think I'm going?'

'If you're going to the toolshed, there's something I want to say to you.'

'Go on.'

'I've spilt a bit of paint – only a little bit, mind – on the door.'

'Don't tell me you've painted the door as well.'

'Only half of it, Daddy. I couldn't reach the top. I wanted to make it all look nice before you came up the garden.'

'That was thoughtful of you.'

'Do you want to go inside the toolshed, Daddy?'

'Certainly. Why not?'

'Well, it might be a bit difficult at the moment. You see, Clare was very naughty and I thought she was going to take her kiddie-car on the main road.'

'Well?'

'Well, Daddy, I used some of those old bricks up the garden. I knew you wouldn't mind because they aren't any good anyhow, to make a barricade.'

'Let's get this clear. Since you have been up the garden this morning, you've found a pot of paint and spread it over yourself, the toolshed door and the kiddie-car.'

'Yes, Daddy.'

'You have now bricked up your sister in the toolshed where she is riding the kiddie-car you have just painted?'

'I told her not to, Daddy.'

'So you've already assured me. As a matter of interest, since you've bricked up the door, how have you yourself been getting in and out of the toolshed?'

'Through the window.'

'But that window won't open.'

'It's open now, Daddy.'

'Do you mean you've broken it?'

'I was coming to that, Daddy. It was an accident. It wasn't me. The boy next door cracked it with his bow and arrow. I told him you'd be very angry.'

'So the boy next door is involved, too.'

'No, Daddy, he's gone home now.'

'And the cracked window?'

'Well, I thought it wasn't much use having a cracked window . . .'

'So you've done the job properly.'

'You can hardly notice it's missing now, Daddy.'

'Is there anything else you want to tell me before I inspect for myself what you've been up to?'

'Oh no, Daddy.'

'You haven't been in the garage, have you?'

'*Only to get the oilcan.*'
'The oilcan?'
'*The kiddie-car needed oil badly.*'
'Did Clare go with you into the garage?'
'*Yes, but I sent her out at once because she climbed into the car.*'
'Did this happen *before* the painting of the kiddie-car; or afterwards?'
'*Afterwards, Daddy.*'
'And *after* Clare had started riding it?'
'*Yes, Daddy.*'
'Go down to the house immediately and ask your mother for some turpentine.'
'*It's O.K., Daddy, I thought you might want it, so I took it up to the toolshed for you.*'

SILLY STORIES

MILES KINGTON

MY FATHER WASN'T much given to handing out philosophy and axioms about life. In fact, I can only remember two occasions on which he came anywhere near generalising about the whole business. The first time was when he said suddenly: 'In my opinion, half the jails in this country are filled with Old Etonians' and the second was when he turned to me and said: 'Miles, never believe anything you hear and only half of what you see. Remember that, and you won't go far wrong.'

It was too late already. Looking back, I can see now that I must have been one of the most gullible children on earth. In the late nineteen-forties, when we were living on the outskirts of Wrexham, my father made me a catapult, lovingly fashioned out of a genuine bit of tree and strong square-cornered elastic which I can feel the touch of to this day. Quite what I was meant to be shooting at I am not sure – I expect Dad just felt that any boy without a catapult wasn't a proper boy – but it was certainly good for showing off to other boys who didn't have catapults.

One of them, to my surprise, was not at all impressed.

'Don't you know that catapults are against the law?' he said.

'Why?' I said.

'They're a dangerous weapon, that's why. They could hurt people seriously. If you're caught with a catapult, the police would probably arrest you.'

Here was a fine mess my father had got me into, I thought.

'What do you think I ought to do?'

'Well,' said the boy, 'perhaps, if we broke it up, it would be all right. A catapult that doesn't work can't be against the law.'

And like an idiot I let him break the catapult in half for me. I went home, feeling very pleased with myself, and told my father that I had saved us all from being arrested. He was absolutely furious and totally unimpressed with my information about the law, which, as I repeated it, did sound rather lame.

And I never learnt from my experience. At about the same time I went out to play one day and became aware of a strange noise I had never heard before. It was a kind of wrenching, searing, grinding noise which came from about a mile away, and it rose and fell in agony. I asked a friend what it was.

'It's the giant.'

'What giant.'

'The giant that's eating up Wrexham. Haven't you heard? It's coming across Wrexham, grinding up everyone's bones and eating them. It's going to be here before nightfall. We're all going to get eaten.'

I believed him utterly. The noise certainly sounded horrible enough. So for the best part of one day, at the age of six, I knew for a fact that I would not survive the night; it is the only time in my life so far when I have been completely convinced that I was on the point of death and that nothing could save me. As far as I can remember, it was a very lonely feeling. But by mid-afternoon I realised that my mother showed no distress at the prospect of being eaten by the giant, so I asked her about the whole sorry business, and suggested that we might run away when Dad came home from work with the car. She didn't know what I was talking about. I took her outside and made her listen to the noise.

'That's the sawmill,' she said. 'It is not a giant. There is no giant. Now run along and don't believe silly stories.'

But I did. For years I went on believing silly stories, whether they were Norse myths, things my schoolfriends told me or tales from the Bible, and it was only gradually over the years that I gave them up, one by one. It's sad, in a way, losing your gullibility. But to compensate for it, I found the delight of telling other people silly stories and seeing them believe you. In fact, come to think of it, I have earned my living by doing it for over twenty years.

I never did find out whether the prisons of Britain are stuffed full of Old Etonians, but I now suspect that they are not.

Even my father told me silly stories.

OPENING THE INNINGS

RACHAEL HEYHOE FLINT

Heyhoe aged 3 – 'Used to scare away the birds in our garden'

MY FIRST BRUSH with the police taught me that, years ago, men had little regard for women cricketers, and my immediate instinct was to register protest. It happened early in my childhood – I think I was eight years old – while I was engaged in my customary tomboy habit of playing cricket with my brother Nicholas and his friends.

The road where I grew up was in a quiet suburb of Wolverhampton, and as there was so little traffic, the road became our sports arena. While the girls of the neighbourhood tended their dolls and prams, I preferred to play bicycle polo – a fraught, high-speed version of the royal's game – and soccer and cricket with the lads.

On this infamous occasion when I brushed with the law, we were some way through an intense cricket match in the road, when one of the local bobbies drove up. He marched towards us as we rushed for cover: aware that our games were at least frowned upon, if not illegal, we scattered to hiding-places behind various trees and hedges. The arm of the law yanked us all out one by one, however, and then out came the black notebook and pencil. He took the names and addresses of all the boys and then went to replace his notebook in his pocket. This was too much for me. I reached up, tapped him on the shoulder and pointed out that I had been playing cricket, too. His answer was most pitying: 'Girls don't play cricket,' which was about as devastating a blow to my pride as anyone could have delivered.

Our house seemed to be adopted as the sporting Mecca by the entire adolescent population of the road, but even when alone, I was never lost for something to do. I

devised my own method of solitary practice, suspending a cricket ball on string from an overhanging plank attached to a low gutter, and patiently drove the ball backwards and forwards until my arms ached and the gutter nearly fell off.

Brother Nicholas and his friends at first tried to exclude me from their back-lawn cricket matches. For some time, I was delegated as preserver of the flower beds. In other words, they deigned to let me field, but refused me the chance to either bat or bowl.

After serving my apprenticeship in the covers, however, they relented and allowed me an innings, presumably with the conviction that it wouldn't last long anyway. I shocked them all by batting undefeated for three days and accumulating a score of about 380 not out. By the end of it, they were so frustrated – I think pride came into it, too – that they declared the opening of the football season and switched games, despite the fact that it was only mid-June.

Being four years older, Nicholas was able to bully little sister quite successfully. But he did, at least, teach me a great deal about courage.

I had to put up with such harrowing indignities as having the vacuum cleaner held over my head so that my plaits were sucked up to the machine. I had to join in crazy 'dares', which included jumping off a twelve-foot-high balcony on to a mattress on our lawn – only when our parents were out, of course.

Nicholas also involved me in his cycle speedway team, which he called the Penn Rockets, and he taught me how to ride a motor-bike. At least, he showed me how to operate clutch, gears and throttle and launched me off over the fields near our home. What he had omitted to explain was how to work the brakes!

Eventually, I became accepted by his mates, almost as one of the gang, although they insisted on nicknaming me Lizzie after that obnoxious Violet Elizabeth Bott in the 'Just William' books who was always threatening to 'scweam and scweam until I'm sick'. To them, I had several uses, not the least important of which involved being sent round to neighbours' houses to retrieve lost cricket balls and footballs, exerting all my feminine charm!

The family on one side of us grew tired of our games and would often refuse to return the ball. But that was almost a relief compared with the house on the other side, where the people were friendly enough but their fearsome vicious bulldog would threaten permanent damage to anyone who set foot on his territory. Duelling with that dog certainly sharpened up my reflexes – as it would have done for anyone whose job it was to bend down and find cricket balls under the rhododendrons with a snarling, snapping creature bearing down on one's seat at a rate of knots.

The garden games involved a simple system of scoring runs, including six if you cleared a fence or hit the house wall on the full or twelve if you cleared the roof. If you broke a window, however, you were out! Not only that, but you also abandoned your part in the game to race into town by bicycle and collect the necessary replacement pane of glass before my parents could discover any damage. I think our

local glazier must have been familiar with every window pane in our house, and several surrounding houses, by the time we had grown up.

When in the sixth form at school I scored the first century of my career. It was against Bilston High School, and I still have the press-cutting to remind me that at one point I struck three sixes and a four in a single over, though admittedly the boundaries were very short. The cutting also reports that it was the first century recorded by a pupil of my school and that I followed it up by taking six wickets for seven runs in the same match. All good, ego-building stuff to reflect on.

Despite my reasonably rapid progress at the game, I retained a very schoolgirlish attitude. In 1955, at sixteen years old, I played my first senior county match for Staffordshire, against Warwickshire. I took six wickets but got myself run out for only seven runs. The most eye-catching feature I found when consulting the match scorecard, however, was the note I had penned in at the top. It reads: 'LUNCH – salad, cheese and biscuits, squash (iced). TEA – sandwiches, lemonade, cream cakes (four).'

from *Heyhoe!*

COMPANIONS IN CORFU

GERALD DURRELL

IN THOSE EARLY days of exploration Roger [the dog] was my constant companion. Together we ventured farther and farther afield, discovering quiet, remote olive-groves which had to be investigated and remembered, working our way through a maze of blackbird-haunted myrtles, venturing into narrow valleys where the cypress-trees cast a cloak of mysterious, inky shadow. He was the perfect companion for an adventure, affectionate without exuberance, brave without being belligerent, intelligent and full of good-humoured tolerance for my eccentricities. If I slipped when climbing a dew-shiny bank, Roger appeared suddenly, gave a snort that sounded like suppressed laughter, a quick look over, a rapid lick of commiseration, shook himself, sneezed and gave me his lop-sided grin. If I found something that interested me – an ant's nest, a caterpillar on a leaf, a spider wrapping up a fly in swaddling clothes of silk – Roger sat down and waited until I had finished examining it. If he thought I was taking too long, he shifted nearer, gave a gentle, whiny yawn, and then sighed deeply and started to wag his tail. If the matter was of no great importance, we would move on, but if it was something absorbing that had to be

pored over, I had only to frown at Roger and he would realise it was going to be a long job. His ears would droop, his tail slow down and stop, and he would slouch off to the nearest bush, fling himself down in the shade, giving me a martyred look as he did so.

During these trips Roger and I came to know and be known by a greater number of people in various parts of the surrounding countryside. There was, for example, a strange, mentally defective youth with a round face as expressionless as a puffball. He was always dressed in tattered shirt, shiny blue serge trousers that were rolled up to the knee, and on his head the elderly remains of a bowler hat without a brim. Whenever he saw us he came hurrying through the olives, raised his absurd hat politely and wished us good day in a voice as childish and sweet as a flute. He would stand, watching us without expression, nodding at any remark I happened to make, for ten minutes or so. Then, raising his hat politely, he would go off through the trees. Then there was the immensely fat and cheerful Agathi, who lived in a tiny tumbledown cottage high up the hill. She was always sitting outside her house with a spindle of sheep's wool, twining and pulling it into coarse thread. She must have been well over seventy, but her hair was still black and lustrous, plaited carefully and wound round a pair of polished cow's horns, an ornament that some of the older peasant women adopted. As she sat in the sun, like a great black toad with a scarlet head-dress draped over the cow's horns, the bobbin of wool would rise and fall, twisting like a top, her fingers busy unravelling and plucking, and her drooping mouth with its hedge of broken and discoloured teeth wide open as she sang, loudly and harshly, but with great vigour.

It was from Agathi that I learnt some of the most beautiful and haunting of the peasant songs. Sitting on an old tin in the sun, eating grapes or pomegranates from her garden, I would sing with her, and she would break off now and then to correct my pronunciation. We sang (verse by verse) the gay, rousing song of the river, *Vangelió*, and of how it dropped from the mountains, making the gardens rich, the fields fertile and the trees heavy with fruit. We sang, rolling our eyes at each other in exaggerated coquetry, the funny little love-song called 'Falsehood.' 'Lies, lies,' we warbled, shaking our heads, 'all lies, but it is my fault for teaching you to go round the countryside telling people I love you.' Then we would strike a mournful note and sing, perhaps, the slow, lilting song called 'Why are you leaving me?' We were almost overcome by this one, and would wail out the long, soulful lyrics, our voices quavering. When we came to the last bit, the most heart-rending of all, Agathi would clasp her hands to her great breasts, her black eyes would become misty and sad, and her chins would tremble with emotion. As the last discordant notes of our duet faded away, she would turn to me, wiping her nose on the corner of her head-dress.

'What fools we are, eh? What fools, sitting here in the sun, singing. And of love, too! I am too old for it and you are too young, and yet we waste our time singing about it. Ah, well, let's have a glass of wine, eh?'

Apart from Agathi, the person I liked best was the old shepherd Yani, a tall, slouching man with a great hooked nose like an eagle, and incredible moustaches. I first met him one hot afternoon when Roger and I had spent an exhausting hour trying to dig a large green lizard out of its hole in a stone wall. At length, unsuccessful, sweaty and tired, we had flung ourselves down beneath five little cypress-trees that cast a neat square of shadow on the sun-bleached grass. Lying there, I heard the gentle, drowsy tinkling of a goat-bell, and presently the herds wandered past us, pausing to stare with vacant yellow eyes, bleat sneeringly and then move on. The soft sound of the bells, and of their mouths ripping and tearing at the undergrowth, had a soothing effect on me, and by the time they had drifted slowly past and the shepherd appeared I was nearly asleep. He stopped and looked at me, leaning heavily on his brown olive-wood stick, his little black eyes, fierce under his shaggy brows, his big boots planted firmly in the heather.

'Good afternoon,' he greeted me gruffly; 'you are the foreigner . . . the little English lord?'

By then I was used to the curious peasant idea that all English people were lords, and I admitted that that's who I was. He turned and roared at a goat which had reared on to its hind legs and was tearing at a young olive, and then turned back.

'I will tell you something, little lord,' he said; 'it is dangerous for you to lie here, beneath these trees.'

I glanced up at the cypresses, but they seemed safe enough to me, and so I asked why he thought they were dangerous.

'Ah, you may *sit* under them, yes. They cast a good shadow, cold as well-water; but that's the trouble, they tempt you to sleep. And you must never, for any reason, sleep beneath a cypress.'

He paused, stroked his moustache, waited for me to ask why, and then went on:

'Why? Why? Because if you did you would be changed when you woke. Yes, the black cypresses, they are dangerous. While you sleep, their roots grow into your brains and steal them, and when you wake up you are mad, head as empty as a whistle.'

I asked whether it was only the cypress that could do this, or did it apply to other trees.

'No, only the cypress,' said the old man, peering up fiercely at the trees above me as though to see whether they were listening; 'only the cypress is the thief of intelligence. So be warned, little lord, and don't sleep here.'

He nodded briefly, gave another fierce glance at the dark blades of the cypress, as if daring them to make some comment, and then picked his way carefully through the myrtle-bushes to where his goats grazed scattered about the hill, their great udders swinging like bagpipes beneath their bellies.

from *My Family and Other Animals*

BLOODY SUNDAY

SIR HUGH CASSON

I WAS BORN IN 1910. My father was in the Indian Civil Service. My mother rightly opted to stay with him in Burma where he was serving, so my sister and I saw them only at rare intervals – one as long as five years. We were brought up by a series of kindly aunts and governesses in a constantly changing series of houses and schools in the company of a constantly changing group of cousins whose parents were similarly placed. To all of us this nomadic and fragmented existence with its weekly letter and annual photograph to parents seemed totally normal and certainly none of us seemed to feel – like Kipling – lonely or unloved. Our childhood in those confident days was secure and mercifully free from disaster. Even the Gotha air raids over Folkstone, where we were living at the time, meant only the minor adventure of sleeping under the piano.

It was however one of those raids that left one vivid visual memory. One Sunday morning we went as usual to church at Hythe. All the way up the long flight of steps from the High Street were drops of blood that had fallen (we were told) the previous night from our friend the verger, killed as he stood within the church porch. The churchyard when we reached it looked in memory like a painting by Stanley Spencer of 'Resurrection' – crooked crosses, fallen headstones, torn turf. I would not have been surprised to see the occupants picking their way over the debris. It was I think the most sharp-edged of all my childhood experiences and the image has not dimmed in memory.

ROYAL ACADEMY OF ARTS,
PICCADILLY, LONDON, W1V 0DS

Telephone: 01-734 9052
Cables: Royacad, London

A LUDLOW CHILDHOOD

P. D. JAMES

ALL MY LIFE I have been fortunate enough to have lived in beautiful places. I was born in Oxford in 1920 but by the time I was five my father, an Inland Revenue official, had moved his family (my mother and a younger sister and brother) to Ludlow on the Welsh borders and it is in this romantic and enchanting little town that I first went to school. The school was the British School, so-called because it was one of the elementary schools originally set up by the British Society, a voluntary society founded in 1840 to promote free education. As I grow older and experience that phenomenon whereby the remote past becomes closer while recent events seem to recede, those early schooldays in Ludlow sixty years ago are fresher in memory than many of my later schooldays.

The day began with morning assembly. We had no hymn books so learned the hymns by heart and I can still hear the Welsh lilt of those childish voices – we were after all near the Welsh border. The young children were expected to press palms closely together and keep their eyes tightly shut during the prayers. The older children, at the back, merely clasped their hands and were permitted to squint at the babies through half-closed lids. These were childish conventions enforced by us not, of course, by the teachers. And the conventions extended to the playground. A special area of asphalt was reserved for the older girls on which they would chalk six square hopscotch patterns for their sole privileged use. Hopscotch was the chief playground game of the girls and much time was spent by the banks of the River Teme finding a smooth stone of exactly the right size and weight, since in our game the stone was kicked and slid from square to square, not thrown. A good hopscotch stone was as valuable a status symbol to a girl as a polished and pickled conker was to a boy.

After English I loved the history lessons best. I suppose we must have been given the sense of historical continuity because I remembered the blue waving River of Time painted on long strips of paper and pinned to the classroom wall. We would draw or cut out figures of Romans, Saxons, Elizabethans and Victorians and paste them in their appropriate dates with clear bridges marking each reign. But my memory of history is of listening enraptured to chronologically disjointed stories, always romantic: snow falling like a white absolving pall on the coffin of Charles the First, the Tolpuddle Martyrs resisting tyranny, Hardy kneeling by the dying body of Nelson, Wolfe scaling the heights of Quebec. History was about glory, tragedy, romance, and for me the subject was so early endowed with these qualities that even when, years later, my history lessons were concerned with Corn Laws, social

legislation and the extension of the franchise, the romance and delight of the subject remained undimmed.

I can't remember a single child at the British School, Ludlow, who left unable to read and write. We learnt our tables by chanting them in unison and practised our hand-writing by copying out over and over again the phrase 'improve each shining hour'. Mr Wynn, the headmaster, imbued us with his love of poetry and his taste was eclectic. I can still recite the poems learnt before I was eight; the Shropshire poems of A.E. Housman and 'The Burial of Sir John Moore after Corunna'.

And then there were the high days; Empire Day when the Union Jack would be run up on a pole in the playground and we would march past saluting it. That day in 1930 when the lone aviator, Amy Johnson, flew solo to Australia and Mr Wynn pinned the map of the world to the blackboard so that we could follow her flight. I remember that map clearly and the large areas coloured red which showed that they were part of the British Empire. We were taught to regard the Empire on which, as the map clearly demonstrated, the sun never set, with respect, awe and great pride and yet, throughout my early childhood, I never saw a brown or black face.

There were splendid places in which to play in Ludlow, and it seems now that life must have been much safer for children. Certainly our parents never worried when we were playing alone round the castle walls, nor was it necessary for us to be escorted to and from school. We used to paddle in the River Teme by the weir and I can remember the day when a child drowned, a memory not, thank God, of the drowning but of being suddenly grasped and borne away by an adult, of hushed voices, of waiting in a huddled group, of being taken home and told nothing.

And yet, in retrospect, how peaceful, how ordered, how gentle that life now seems. Yet it had its tragedies. Scarlet fever, usually called 'the fever', could kill and often did, and diphtheria was a dreaded word. During epidemics the school would be closed and then fumigated before we reassembled. And I can remember poverty among my playmates which I don't see today; the torn, inadequate clothing, the shoes which barely held together, the thin arms trembling in winter with the cold. I can even recall the name, George, of one small boy who invariably came to school almost ragged and clutching an unbuttered crust which was his breakfast. I remember, too, the visit of the nit-nurse and the misery and shame of those children whose heads were found to be infected and who were handed a letter to their parents in full view of us all. We were a mixed bunch, children from the prosperous middle-class and from the desperate poor. And yet during the whole of my primary schooling I never knew of a theft at school or saw a policeman.

And then there was the dreaded day of the scholarship examination, the result of which would determine whether the child was one of a privileged few to be awarded a place at the Girls' High School or the Boys' Grammar School or would go with the great majority to the National School. Only those few children whose parents could afford to pay the fees were spared this ordeal. I got close to success, but

not close enough, let down as always by my inability to do arithmetic. If I had succeeded in that test before I was eleven I might eventually have had the university education I always wanted. Would I have been a better writer, I wonder, with the benefit of that more rigorous academic training, or even a writer at all?

SNAPSHOTS

ROBERT ROBINSON

One of 'The Two Terrors of the Known World'

THERE WAS THE lane and the brook and the fields. Our house was on the corner – of the world, I used to think. My Dad opened the camera and pulled out the black concertina part. He put the palm of his hand round the little glass cube in which he saw the picture, and pulled the lever down slowly with his thumb. I was standing under the apple-tree. When my Dad looked up at me after he took the picture, I knew we were going to live for ever.

One of the first things I ever did was walk out of the back gate and hold one arm up and the other arm out, like a policeman. A boy pedalling along in a toy car stopped. After that he was my best friend, his name was Bob Russell. Then there were the two Margarets, and Keith, and Mrs de Cruise and Mr Parish and Dr Roberts. One time, Bob and I got lost – we went off in our toy cars (his was blue and made of wood, mine was red and made of tin) and when we came back we were singing. 'At the top of their voices!' cried all the grown-ups, half appalled, half in admiration. That was when Dr Roberts called us The Two Terrors of The Known World.

The Avenue ran down the side of our long garden, and was in a constant state of being re-surfaced. The tar was like treacle and the grit the steamroller pressed into it was crunchy when you walked over it, like almonds. When we played cricket, if the

ball went over the fence into the Avenue, it was six and out. Sometimes my Mum would stop doing the washing-up and come out on a Spring evening when it was getting along towards dusk, and insist on having a go at batting. I was ashamed of the way she held the bat with one hand, but proud of the way she hit out contemptuously at the ball and walloped it over the fence.

When I fell into the brook Bob Russell walked home behind me holding up my new overcoat as it dripped with green slime. I fell out of the apple-tree, and landed on my back across the garden-roller, and knocked all the breath out of my body, and it was the way I couldn't start to breathe again that impressed both the Margarets (who'd seen it happen) and Keith who had been told about it. Then one Guy Fawkes Night they all came into our garden and my Dad was just putting a rocket into a milk bottle when Bob lit a sparkler and dropped it into the big box my Dad had put the fireworks in, and they all went off at once. Both the Margarets burst into tears, but it was terrible the way Bob held out the two jumping-jacks and the boy-scout rouser he'd brought with him, and begged me to set them on fire. My Dad said a bit sourly, 'If Bob Russell cut your head off, I think you'd forgive him.'

We tormented my grand-dad. My Mum sent him out to haul us in, in the evenings, when we were the other side of the brook and deep in the fields. We'd spot him and shout 'Grand-dad!', and dodge down behind the overgrown bunkers left over from when the fields had been a golf-course. Then he'd give up, and we'd follow him home, shouting after him, and hiding, until he wouldn't turn round any longer. Once we locked him in the outside lavatory, once we pushed him on to a bonfire in the garden, once we chucked his hat into the brook. When he was reading I'd stand on the rung of the chair behind him and wrinkle up his bald head with my fingers. 'Mad bugger' he'd say, without looking up from the page.

Next door to me was the first Margaret, then there was Keith, then there was a young man called Bernard who was twenty and taught at the Sunday School and when I was three-and-a-half I didn't know why his mother laughed when I knocked at his door and asked if Bernard wanted to come out to play. Then there was Bob and the other Margaret, who was his sister. And then Mrs de Cruise. She had a handsome grown-up daughter who taught tap-dancing to little girls in the church-hall. When we bent down, peeping through the keyhole to see her in her tights, she suddenly opened the door. 'Cheek!' she magnificently cried, as we raced away.

Where are we all now? Why, still there. The snapshots are imperishable. Sometimes I try and return, but the place no longer has a location, it's not on the map. I feel perverse, making an actual journey to a place I can't ever leave.

FAIRY TALES

BARBARA CARTLAND

Taking the air at Hatfield

PERSHORE, WORCESTERSHIRE
·1907·

I AM WALKING along a country road holding onto the perambulator which my nanny is pushing. Inside it is my new baby brother Ronald who was born in January.

I am very bored with having him with us and have already said to my mother:

'Mummy, do let us send that baby away. Everyone asks after him and no one asks after me!'

I think the real reason I resent him is that my mother looks at him in a different way from how she looks at me. Her eyes seem to have a light behind them and her voice is full of love.

I know now I am not part of her as I was before, but complete in myself, and I feel alone. Even when people are all round me I am alone and it's a strange and rather frightening feeling.

We reach a cottage where Nanny is to leave some soup for a woman who is ill. While she talks at the door I cross the road.

There is a gate into the park which is open.

I stand beside it and look at the crimson poppies among the grasses, the purple cuckoo-flowers, the white and gold marguerites, and the blue love-in-the-mist.

Suddenly, as I am looking at them, the flowers seem to come nearer to me, to get larger . . . and larger.

There is a strange vibration coming from them and I think that I can see them growing . . . living . . . breathing . . .

It is so extraordinary and so exciting that I stand staring at the flowers and I know they are alive as I am.

'Barbara!' It is my nanny's voice. 'What are you doing? Come here at once, you naughty little girl!'

The spell is broken, I run back across the road . . .

· 1910 ·

I know there are goblins with huge heads and little bodies burrowing beneath the hills.

There are nymphs soft as the mist in the silver lakes and streams; huge green dragons, fighting and breathing fire, lurk in the darkness of the pine woods.

There are two big trees very close together in the secret part of the garden, and when I am going to sleep I know that if I can squeeze between them I shall find all that I am seeking, although I am not certain what it is.

Sometimes I have a glimpse of a fairy amongst the flowers – I see her out of the corner of my eye, but when I turn my head she has gone.

The fairies dance on the lawn at night and leave a circle of mushrooms; so I know they have been there.

In the winter when the leafless branches of the trees are silhouetted against the sunset, I have a strange feeling within me, as if they lift me up into the sky.

· 1912 ·

I have read *Alice Through the Looking-Glass* and I know now that what I have been trying to do before I go to sleep is to step through the Looking-Glass.

That is the world that fascinates and draws me, the world I sense between the trees, the world of the Goblins and Fairies, a world behind the world.

I know it is very near me, a shadow behind my head, just round the corner, at the top of the stairs.

I am determined to find it.

Sometimes when I am alone in the garden I put my ear against the trunk of a tree. I can hear it breathing and living. Everything has life in it like the life in me.

But there is another part of life which I cannot hear or touch, yet it is there through the Looking-Glass.

MUSIC AND LAUGHTER

JIMMY YOUNG

TO TELL THE truth, I can't remember very much about what went on when I was young. The main reason for that, I suppose, is that my childhood seems, as the song title puts it, 'Long ago and far away'.

And yet the very fact that I use a song title within my first two sentences pinpoints the one love which was an overwhelming influence on my childhood. That love was music.

I was born in a little mining town in Gloucestershire called Cinderford, at a time when there was very little money about and, in consequence, times were hard. However, it doesn't cost money to sing, and we all know how marvellous the miners' male voice choirs sound. Singing cheers you up and warms you up at the same time. Which may sound a bit like a television commercial, but is true.

Both my parents came from musical families. My father sang in male voice choirs. My mother sang, and also played both the piano and the organ. She began playing the organ in the local church at the age of seven, and continued to do so for the next seventy-three years! When she was eighty she turned to me one day and said, 'You know, son, I really think I ought to give up and make way for someone a little younger.'

She also taught the piano, and was instructing pupils right up to three days before she died, in June 1972. She, of course, taught me to play piano and to read music. Indeed I could read music before I could read!

My grandfather married twice and, including adoptions, accumulated a family of sixteen children. Most of those children had also had children, so you can imagine that we were a very large tribe. And since they all sang as well, we were a very noisy tribe into the bargain.

Music and Christmas time. They are the two things I most easily remember from my childhood.

All us kids together at Christmas time. There seemed to be millions of us. And since there was no telly we made our own entertainment. Parlour games, blow football on the kitchen table, and always the piano going. Laughter and music, those are the things that come flooding back.

It was those experiences, all those years ago, that told me with absolute certainty what it was I wanted to do in life. I am extremely grateful for my family background because, looking back, I know that was when the seeds were planted that pointed me in the direction I wanted to go.

PLAYING THE GAME

KEITH WATERHOUSE

I ARRIVED AT my council elementary school on a Leeds housing estate a precocious four-year-old and left it a precocious fourteen-year-old.

In the intervening years I was intolerable. I went through my schooldays convinced that I was the cleverest boy in the school – which, if cunning is another word for cleverness, I was.

I was astounded and hurt if I did not come top in examinations, for I was a brilliant and audacious cheat. For conventional studies I had no time at all. My only aim was to demonstrate my superiority over all those who were ill-starred enough to be my teachers, whom I arrogantly regarded as morons. It is astonishing I survived.

I was allowed to join the infants' class two terms early by reason of having harassed my mother to distraction by prematurely reading books. A self-taught four-year-old among a class of five-year-old illiterates is off to a head start. No wonder I was insufferable.

I won my first school prize at the age of six. Our teacher, a Miss Pease, turned up on the first day of term with a ceramic salt, pepper and mustard set in the form of a donkey and fruit-cart. I don't know how she came by it or what possessed her to offer a cruet as a suitable prize for children barely weaned off rusks. But offer it she did. It was to go to the boy or girl judged by Miss Pease to have been the best-behaved during the term. I determined to have it.

So did all the other children in the class (so maybe it was not such a bizarre choice after all). But I was smarter than they were. I reasoned that being of such tender years they would quickly forget why they were behaving so nauseatingly well, and would lapse into their old ways. I, however, would remember. Instead of wasting my energies being indistinguishably well-behaved along with everyone else, I would continue routinely creating havoc until the last couple of weeks of term, by which time all my classmates would have fallen by the wayside. I would then bring myself to Miss Pease's attention with a quick spurt of angelic behaviour, and so win the prize. The ploy worked. I bore the donkey-and-cart cruet home with smug pride and it stood on my mother's mantelpiece for twenty-five years.

Moving up to the junior school was an unsettling experience, for the junior school had male teachers, many of them said to be of a violent disposition, and I was not sure that they were to be bamboozled as easily as the ladies in lilac smocks I had led by the nose in my spectacular career in kindergarten.

I decided to put the issue to the test at the earliest opportunity. Positioning

myself outside the junior school staff-room, I chalked on the wall in six-inch-high letters the legend KW IS A FOOL. And then waited for a teacher to emerge. As it happened, it was the headmaster himself who came out first. Quailing inwardly, I regarded him unblinkingly as he stared distastefully at my graffiti.

'Is that your handiwork, boy?'

'No, sir.'

'Don't lie to me, laddie! You still have the chalk in your hand!'

'But sir!' I piped up, all injured innocence, pointing to the KW in KW IS A FOOL. 'Those are my own initials. I'm not likely to call myself a fool, am I?' Thwarted by this piece of warped logic, the headmaster strode off without another word. Brandishing my chalk, I turned back to my handiwork and thickly underlined it for good measure, assessing correctly that he wouldn't remember whether it had been underlined or not.

Waterhouse at large

In junior school I learned how to win at exams. The more spectacular the crib, I found, the less likely it was to be detected. Teachers were always on the look-out for history dates scribbled on thumb-nails or on bits of stamp-hinging wrapped around inkwells. They were not on the look-out for history dates meticulously copied out to resemble a school timetable and then pinned to the class notice-board – which happened to be next to my desk. I put no little effort into cheating at exams – far more than I ever did into swotting up for them – and I regret to say that I have never felt the slightest twinge of guilt at thus beating classmates academically abler than myself.

My most famous coup was to cause an end-of-term geography paper to be 'lost', so that I had to sit the examination again. By that time, of course, I had mugged up the answers. But to allay suspicion I was careful not to get every one right, so that I came not top, but third. Such subtle manoeuvres, while doing little for the soul, must at least have been useful for exercising the intellect. More fruitful, I believe, than learning the principal rivers of Australia.

I think I will draw a veil over my three years in senior school. I was bolshie, cocky, overwhelmingly conceited and a considerable pain in the neck, especially to my English teacher, with whom I used to argue insolently about syntax. Probably to his relief, I discovered the delights of playing hookey. A playground fall had resulted in my having to report to the City Infirmary for a series of X-rays, and I had had the foresight to retain the last of my official appointment cards demanding my presence on Friday at 3pm. But it didn't say which Friday. Over a period of two years, brandishing my grubby exeat, I would periodically skip Friday afternoon English classes and take myself off to the pictures.

Years later, when as a reporter on the local paper I went back to my school to cover some function or other, I confessed to my English teacher.

'Yes, I know,' he said. 'You were seen more than once going into the cinema.'

'Then why didn't you do anything about it?'

'We didn't want to cramp your style,' he said. And it wasn't until then that I realised my teachers knew more than I thought about teaching.

from *Waterhouse at Large*

HIGH IN THE ALPS

LORD HUNT

I HAVE A vivid memory of my first visit to Switzerland – indeed, it was my first sight of mountains – as a child of ten. Travel in Europe was very cheap for British holiday-makers shortly after the First World War; I seem to recall that my mother paid seven Swiss francs for full board in a *pension* above Lake Geneva when the pound sterling was worth twenty-five francs. That was in 1920. However that may be, and despite being a war widow with very few resources other than my father's pension, she contrived to take my brother and myself to the Alps for winter as well as summer holidays for the next ten years. This may explain my love of mountains and my passion for mountaineering and skiing.

Apart from brief and incidental mental snapshots during the war years, my earliest clear memory is of the Château de Chillon, beside the Lake Geneva, with a shapely if modest mountain in the background: the Dents du Midi. It is a scene made familiar to countless other people who may never have been there, by a picture on boxes of Swiss chocolate. Perhaps it was that mountain which sowed in my youthful mind the seed of ambition to climb.

But the impressions of childhood are focused mainly on the foreground; only dimly was I aware of that distant and seemingly inaccessible peak. I remember a picnic in a meadow somewhere high above the lake, on an *alp* rich with wild flowers over which butterflies and grasshoppers were flitting. I also remember the occasion because a Swiss friend accompanied us; he was the head of the famous firm of chocolate manufacturers: Suchard. So you may understand that my interest in Switzerland was not confined to the picture on the chocolate box!

Switzerland was a source of inspiration for some of our great romantic poets in the early part of the nineteenth century. Byron wrote a poem entitled 'Evening on Lake Geneva' while he was in a rowing boat on the lake, which appears in *Childe Harold's Pilgrimage* and evokes my own feelings as a child:

> *It is the hush of night, and all between*
> *The margin and the mountains, dusk, yet clear,*
> *Mellowed and mingling, yet distinctly seen,*
> *Save darkn'd Jura, whose capt heights appear*
> *Precipitously steep: and drawing near, there*
> *Breathes a living fragrance from the shore,*
> *Of flowers yet fresh with childhood: on the ear*
> *Drops the light drip of the suspended oar,*
> *Or chirps the grasshopper one goodnight carol more.*

John Hunt second from left – future leader of the first expedition to conquer Mt Everest

SNOWFRUTE AND SHELTERS

CLAIRE RAYNER

Family trio, Claire on the left

To BE BORN in 1931 was a grave error of judgement. The Depression was at its trough (one can hardly refer to its height) and that meant short commons in every department of life. Until I learned to read at five I thought 'Ican'taffordit' was just one word, a long, grown-up way round to say 'no' to a request for a ha'penny half of a Walls' Snowfrute ('Stop me and buy one!' commanded the men in peaked hats who trundled through our East End of London streets, on sit-up-and-beg tricycles with ice boxes on the front, and how I yearned to do as I was bid!). I also thought that every person in the world bought scraps of cloth at market stalls to sew into scratchy knickers for children to suffer, and that having feet that hurt because you'd outgrown your shoes was the way things were supposed to be.

And then the War happened, and everything changed overnight. They told me first of all that Mr Manners was dead. He was the invisible person for whom you always had to leave a tiny bit of your dinner on the side of your plate. It was especially important to do so if it was a dinner you liked, such as mashed potatoes with baked beans in pink goo. It was wicked not to eat everything you were given, but just as wicked not to leave some for Mr Manners; especially when it was dinners

you didn't like, such as boiled fat mutton and cabbage; life was very confusing for children then. But once the war came, Mr Manners was dead, so we didn't have to leave any food anymore. It was just plain evil to leave so much as half a bean on your plate, as wicked as picking your nose or sticking your tongue out at grown-ups. All such behaviour destined you for hellfires, of which we were told a great deal, as I recall, by earnest teachers in glasses and hair thinly waved like the iron roofs on the backyard lavvies all down our street, and harassed mothers who never stopped frowning.

But Mr Manners' demise was not the only change. There was the way the sky suddenly sprouted barrage balloons with glimmering rainbows around their fat tails, and all the street lights went out and backyards were dug up and fitted with holes with roofs called shelters. The shelters smelled of carbolic and cats (you couldn't keep them out) and oil lamps and, within a very few weeks, of mildew. To this day I find the smell of mildew deeply nostalgic and reassuring. And then the streets changed, filling up with men in dirty brown suits and silly little hats perched sideways on their heads, and the wireless changed and all day long there was just Sandy McPherson playing the theatre organ, and school changed as all the other children were evacuated, and then the world changed as I was evacuated.

Not for long though. I became an adept at running away. Within days of arriving In The Country I would sniff out the nearest railway station and go and hide on trains (I was small enough then to flatten myself behind lavatory doors and avoid being caught by ticket collectors) and would get myself home, back to the streets and mildewed shelters and all that made life normal. They kept on evacuating me, of course, trying to convince me it was For My Own Good (yes, they told children all the same things then as they do now) which of course I knew to be nonsense, so I kept on running away, and eventually they gave up and let me stay in London. And then the biggest change of all happened and I was buried in a raid, because I had broken my promise not to go anywhere dangerous, and had taken a short cut across a patch of rubble and . . . but that is another story.

As I said, to be born in 1931 was really rather daft. Because after the war came Growing Up and, at precisely the same time, Austerity. Which meant pretty well the Depression all over again, only several times worse. Now it wasn't just 'Ican'taffordit' but also 'Ihaven'tgotthecoupons' and by the time that was over and the Festival of Britain had arrived and with it the first teenagers who wore special clothes and had special teenage high old jinks, I was too old. I'd done my growing up and missed all that fun. And because of my original bad timing, when the Swinging Sixties arrived, I was up to my ears – or certainly some part of my anatomy – in Motherhood. I spent that delirious decade either pregnant or murmuring 'later, darling – just let me get the baby changed . . .'

Ah well, next time I'll choose a better year to make my entrance centre stage. I quite fancy 3003. It sounds so much shapelier than awkward old 1931.

LOVE BENEATH THE TABLE

BRYAN FORBES

IT WAS LOVE beneath the table – dark, unrequited, innocent. I could only have been four years old at the time, possibly even younger, for although my earliest recollections go even farther back and I can recall the pain and panic of a serious, near fatal illness before the age of two, the remembered shadows on the nursery wall are thrown by brief candles and the early flame is not steady or reliable.

To say I fell in love is to exaggerate an unformed emotion with the hindsight of nearly sixty years. But it was a passion, and I can remember turning to it time and time again like a drug.

The object of my love was a photograph of an unknown little girl of my own age running naked along the edge of the sea. There is no point in concealing that my attraction to her was entirely physical, for she was a very *naked* naked little girl, and I have never ceased to be thankful to her. She was one of the illustrations in *The Glaxo Baby Book*, a publication given away to regular purchasers of that admirable product. I believe I can claim to have been a 'Glaxo Baby' as they were glowingly termed in the adverts. Certainly I wasn't breast-fed, and my mother later confessed that I was not a welcome pregnancy. She conceived me somewhat late in life. I was born in 1926 in the sullen aftermath of the General Strike in my mother's forty-first year and some six years after the birth of my only sister, Betty. Although memory was strongly diluted by pride, to the end of her days my mother frequently returned to a much-polished monologue – chronicling a long and painful labour in Queen Mary's Hospital, Stratford-atte-Bow, which is literally within sound of the fabled Cockney bells. It was there during a night thunderstorm that I claimed identity on the 22nd July 1926, which places me, in horoscopic terms, leaving Cancer and at the cusp of Leo.

The love-affair started in that back room at 43 Cranmer Road, Forest Gate, where I spent the first thirteen years of my childhood. I remember crawling under the dark, tasselled tablecloth, careful not to disturb my maternal grandmother who always sat to the left of the black coal range and who remained dozingly unaware of my illicit practices. Once concealed beneath the table I would turn to that page, and that page only, and gaze upon my beloved. In retrospect I can conjure guilt across the years – but was it really guilt, I wonder? Are we born with such prudery, or is it only the smear that forty years of living has thumbed on to the subconscious?

Beyond the safety of the tablecloth Grandma Seaton, deaf and devoted to me, remained convinced of my innocence in all matters. I must have had a certain basic cunning, for I committed all my acts of love and rebellion while she was asleep, sometimes turning out the entire contents of my father's desk, a crime which he treated as on a level with the Nazi reoccupation of the Rhineland. When awake she would roll dusters into a ball for me and throw them, her chuckling face in shadow, tears of laughter glistening on her old cheeks – a phenomenon which more than anything else about her always fascinated me, I remember. I would stand very close to her chair peering up into her lined face while the tears coursed silently down, for all the world like the end of a drought travelling across parched earth. And then, suddenly, in the midst of laughter, she would lapse back into sleep, her head falling forward with an abruptness that, to a child, seemed like death: as though invisible hands had snapped her neck. She was in her nineties, a farmer's daughter and a farmer's wife from Gedney Hill, Lincolnshire, the mother of nine boys and four girls.

I would back away from her when this happened, unsure but not afraid, and stand motionless at the other end of the room, seeking to solve the many mysteries of somebody so old, so unknown. Then, when convinced that the game was postponed, I would stealthily remove *The Glaxo Baby Book* from the cupboard on the other side of the hearth and take it to my lair. Safe beneath the table again, I would turn once more to the favourite page, amazed every time that the object of my passion was still excitingly the same. I kissed that page, kissed the naked image until the imprint of my lips stained the sepia-tinted shiny paper. The little naked girl had fair, curly hair, I remember, and was running from left to right along the edge of an unknown sea. I loved her beyond recall and included her in my prayers. I loved her until the book disintegrated, and then I forgot her.

from *Notes for a Life*

THE SCHOLARSHIP

LYNDA LEE-POTTER

Peggy Berry's girl

IT WAS CALLED the scholarship and for a whole year it was the main topic of conversation in the council house where I grew up in the mining village of Leigh. The scholarship was the door to the grammar school, to freedom, to the road that meant I'd never have to work in the Trueform shoe shop where my mother spent the first few years of her working life. She was devastatingly pretty, with thick curly hair and shapely legs which she liked to show off in fiendishly high heels. She wore them every day, even on Fridays and Saturdays when the shop was open till ten at night. At the end of a thirteen-hour working day, she'd go home and soak her feet in a bucket of hot water because they ached so much. The shop was perishingly cold and she suffered from chilblains for the rest of her life.

There was no bathroom in my grandad's house in Gordon Street and no electricity, but her sister used to make her exquisitely stylish clothes and heads always turned as she walked down the street.

She cared terribly how I looked, but I was fat and freckled and very plain with fine straight hair. All my childhood I can remember people I didn't know coming up to me and saying, 'You're Peggy Berry's girl, aren't you? What a shame you're not pretty like your mother.' I felt terribly guilty about it as though I'd let her down somehow.

She loved me totally and she was always trying to fight nature. When money was so short she could scarcely find the nine shillings and sixpence weekly rent, she somehow saved up enough to arrange for me to be probably the first child to have what was then known as 'a permanent wave' in Lancashire. It took hours in the front room of a hairdresser two streets away. I was wired up to one of those six-foot perming machines and left there for hours. Every night my mother rolled up the resultant frizz in rags, put lemon juice on my freckles, and still this large rather angry-looking face shone truculently out at the world.

She'd look at me with an amalgam of love and despair, but she never gave up and I was subjected to every beauty hint on record. Her own mother had died soon after she was born, she had no model to base her maternal skills on but her commitment to me was forever. Nothing was too good for me, no ambition too far fetched, no goal

too remote; but the scholarship, later to be called the eleven plus, had to be won first. If I didn't get that then there was little she could do.

For months beforehand we talked of nothing else. She'd think up endless titles for compositions I might be set. We did extra sums after school. She'd had limited schooling but she had a naturally agile mathematical brain and she could reckon up a column of figures like a computer.

The dress I was to wear on that fateful day was washed and ironed weeks in advance. On the Saturday morning neither of us could eat, but we had a cup of hot sweet tea. 'Give it all you've got, love,' she said and there were tears in her eyes.

The school where the exam was to be held was two miles away and I walked there with three other girls in our street.

I sat down and looked at the title of the composition which was where my greatest hope of success rested. To this day I can remember the sick horror I felt when I saw the dreary unimaginative title. 'Write a composition' it said 'on the difference between an apple and an orange.'

Three months later I got a letter telling me I'd passed. I think it was the happiest day of my mother's life.

FINDING FATHER

JOHN ARLOTT

'DAD' WAS A distant, unknown, but romantic figure; remembered in prayers but encountered only in talk with Mum and Grandfather; never consciously seen. When he went to the First World War in 1915, he left behind a one-year-old son. He was sent to Palestine, Mesopotamia and India; but home leave, then, was an unheard of luxury for a private soldier – and if ever there was a tragi-comic misnomer it was 'private' in that context. Even when the war ended there were many duties to be carried out and, in addition – and even decisively – troop ships were few and far between.

So 1918 came – and armistice, with its relief from anxiety for families – and 1919 arrived, but still no 'Dad': only the regular letters with their separated section 'My dear son'.

No such luxury as cables for men on a shilling a day; but the letters never wavered. One day, too, came the news 'They say we shall be coming home soon; so, if you don't hear from me for a few days, that will mean I am on board ship.' Soon,

too, the postmarks and then the stamps bore witness to a steady eastward progress.

The most vivid of all childhood memories are of those daily walks to the station. Although some of the troop trains from Southampton, where his ship would probably land, simply thundered through on the way to London, a number pulled into Basingstoke station – usually, no doubt because of demobilisation procedures, and the relative shortness of the journey, in late afternoon. The walk became a daily routine, hurry home from school – a new experience – and down to the station with Mum. The platform would be crowded with hopeful women, who surged forward as the train stopped and then sadly drew back as their hopes evaporated. Many of them, though, put a cheerful face on their disappointment by buying cups of tea for those lucky ones on the train; and shared the reflected joy of the wives and mothers whose men had arrived. Occasionally, some of the elated train passengers on their way home would celebrate with wild whoops and a countdown which culminated in all the cups being thrown on to the platform and smashed. Then, with Mum's forcedly cheerful 'Ah well, he'll probably come tomorrow', the determined plod home to the tea prepared for his homecoming – which cheered one small boy with cake consumed regularly lest, when he did come, it might be stale.

The day came. 'It's him; *oh*, Jack,' cried Mum as the two ran along with the train to keep up with the man from the photographs, with his moustache and tunic, who was leaning out of the window. He leapt out, kissed Mum, held his son briefly at arm's length as if to survey him, and then took them both in his arms as the mates, most of whom he would never see again, shouted 'All right, Jack, we'll get your kit out': and there, all of a sudden, it was, on the platform beside the huddled group where two had become three. That hug, with all its odd, new smells – pipe tobacco, khaki, button polish – the kiss with a moustache, was for ever imprinted; so were Mum's tears – and Dad's. 'All right, my lad'll bring your stuff round,' said a friendly, elderly porter. 'Oh, thanks, thanks.' Slowly the three made their way home; their speech alternately bubbling and murmured. Life for the three had changed; Mum had her Jack again, he had his wife again and a virtually new son, who could now match the other boys: he had a dad.

ONE OF THE ROUGHEST

BILL BEAUMONT

At the age of four I found that all good things come to an end – I started school. The first stage of my education took place at an establishment with the most unpretentious of names – it was simply called the Council School. Every child has his or her favourite time at school and I was no exception. I thoroughly enjoyed the breaks. When the bell sounded for a break, we would rush out into the playground and play soccer until the next bell tolled to summon us back to the grim realities of the classroom. From all the evidence I've been able to collect from parents, teachers, and the end-of-year reports, there seemed very little danger of my turning into a book worm or an academic recluse. My appetite for such exciting adventures as the alphabet and addition and subtraction was strictly limited and I was not particularly skilful at disguising my lack of interest in such pursuits.

In the hope that I might expand my educational horizons beyond a useful working knowledge of the game of soccer, my parents decided to send me when I was eight years old to a prep school – Cressbrook School in Kirkby Lonsdale.

My father took me along for my interview at Cressbrook and that was the first time I ever touched a rugby ball. I spotted a large wicker basket full of balls outside the headmaster's study and took this as a healthy sign of the shape of things to come. I picked one up and, as the headmaster, Mr David Donald, came out of his room, hastily threw it back into the basket. He took my interest in the rugby ball as an encouraging sign. By getting my name right, I sailed through the interview.

My abiding memory of the school was being forced to have a cold bath every morning throughout the winter and spring terms. In the summer term, glory be, we had the thrilling dilemma of choosing either a cold bath or swimming a length of the freezing outdoor swimming pool. As if that was not enough, the school also had the perverse fetish of embarking regularly on long cross-country walks. I arrived at the school on a Friday and on the Saturday, after, of course, my cold bath, I was dragged six miles across fields, over hills and down dales. I wondered what the blazes was going on.

Surprisingly, although my system never quite accepted the cruel shock of the cold bath every morning, I enjoyed my days at Cressbrook School enormously, with its strong emphasis on the outdoor life and sport. The head boy at the school when I arrived was a blond-haired boy called John Spencer. We all lived in his reflected glory during the next few years as he went on to play for Sedbergh, England Schoolboys, Cambridge University and, eventually, England.

Initially, we played soccer in the autumn and rugby in the spring term, but later on we concentrated on rugby right through the winter. The master in charge of the

rugby side in my first season went on the shrewd principle that the eight biggest lads were made into forwards and the other seven became backs. Thus, I spent the term as a prop forward, although by the end of it I realised there must be a more glamorous position in which I could play. The next season, would you believe, the fly half of the Cressbrook School Juniors was W.B. Beaumont.

In my final year at Cressbrook I was made captain of the rugby team, but I only played a couple of matches before breaking an ankle. This accident, it will be noted, did not occur in the school library by my falling off a ladder trying to reach a book on the top shelf in vigorous pursuit of my studies. I was no more enthusiastic to eat from the tree of knowledge than I had been hitherto, but none the less I was making satisfactory progress. My comeback to the games field was unfortunately delayed because I broke the plaster on my leg while playing yet another impromptu game of soccer on the tennis court. Nothing so trivial as a broken leg was allowed to curtail my sporting activities.

I went to Wembley to watch my first major sporting event – a soccer international in which England beat Scotland by a small matter of nine goals to three. My next big treat was in my last year at Cressbrook when our rugby side had an away match in Edinburgh on the Friday afternoon before the Calcutta Cup match. It was quite an occasion for a bunch of youngsters to set off for the first time in their lives to a real away match played in a foreign country, stay overnight in a hotel, and watch a live rugby international. We arrived at Murrayfield at midday on the Saturday and plonked ourselves down on our seats in the enclosure, soaking up the atmosphere for three hours until the kick-off.

I relished every moment and it made a deep impression on me, although never for a second did I ever dream that one day I would play an international on that pitch. I did have the audacity to dream in my more romantic moments that one day, perhaps, Boycott and Beaumont would open for England at Old Trafford, but there was precious little conviction behind the fantasy. The only black spot on a wonderful day was the result at Murrayfield – Scotland won by 15 points to 6 – and that put a mild damper on the return journey.

In 1965, at the end of a lively and interesting period of my life, the time had come to leave Cressbrook. The headmaster told my parents that I would be remembered as one of the roughest, toughest boys to have passed through the school. He added, 'Roughest in the nicest possible way, of course' – whatever that meant. He said I was one of those unfortunate wretches that trouble seemed to court. Through no fault of my own, trouble tended to follow me around. I recall explaining to him one day that it was just desperately bad luck that I happened to be leaning against the huge plate-glass window of the local sweet shop when it splintered into a thousand pieces and I plunged through the gap. It could have happened to anyone.

from *Thanks to Rugby*

RATS, RABBITS AND REVIVALISTS

SIR ALASTAIR BURNET

MY CHILDHOOD WAS simple and uncomplicated, until I went away to school. We didn't have too much money, but we didn't have too little. Church-going was important, and so was Sunday school, and, of course, we walked there in all weathers; the battery wireless was listened to for serious things, not entertainment; and the papers we took (I am not sure how much they were read) were the *Glasgow Herald* and the *Daily Telegraph*.

Not that until 1938, when I was ten, the outside world impinged at all on my consciousness. A holiday abroad was not thought of. When ordered to write a short essay on Hitler I had to confess I had not heard of him, and was allowed, disparagingly, to write about house painting instead. The economic slump chiefly passed me by, though I remember being taken to see the huge Cunarder sitting unfinished on the stocks at Clydebank while the shops in the streets around seemed filled with the tools the John Brown men had pawned or sold to keep their families going.

In Easter Ross, where my mother and I spent every summer before the war with my great-aunt Eliza on her croft, pleasures had to be simple, water was pumped by hand from the well, and there was only one kerosene lamp in the kitchen; we went to bed by candlelight. My great-aunt had a horse called Tommy and a cow called Nancy, whose annual calf was sold off, with all of us in tears, each autumn. We still cut the edges of the corn fields by scythe before the binder could be let loose, and the dogs and I waited excitedly as the last small square was cut for the desperate rush of the rabbits and rats trapped inside it. That was hot work, and much preferable to snaring: the creatures caught would cry for ages at night.

The sun certainly didn't always shine: the rain actually seemed heaviest in the tattie-howking (potato-picking) season when the world was reduced to one cold, muddy morass and fingers that were numb. Nearby was a great estate gone to rack and ruin. Its owner could not, or would not, pay his taxes, so his silos stank with the rotting harvest of five years before, and the grasses grew too tall in the fields for cattle to eat.

The nearest neighbour on the other side was a road mender (although there was small evidence of his sporadic efforts among the pot-holes) who made his porridge on Saturday evening, poured out seven plates of it and put them in a chest of drawers (I

watched him through the window) so that he could breakfast off one, cold and curling, each morning.

Our little church was made of corrugated iron (the rival one, the old parish church, had been won by the Wee Frees in a famous court case, taken to the House of Lords, so we didn't think much of the Lords), and whenever it rained the din from the roof drowned out the organ.

Drink, naturally, was frowned on, and leave of absence to thirsty male relatives to go the six miles to the nearest place of refreshment was rarely given. It was in such circumstances that an uncle surprisingly volunteered to take the boy to a revivalist meeting (such were our diversions) at the nearest village. He had counted on the saving of souls being over decently before closing time. As the minutes ticked away he gripped my hand and, bending down to get his cap and coat, whispered to me: 'Let's get out of this, man.' The revivalist, a keen-sighted individual, thought he was praying.

'Brother, brother,' he cried triumphantly, 'have you found Christ?'

'I wish to Christ,' my uncle declared fiercely, 'I could find my bunnet.'

This was duly reported by much of the audience to my great-aunt. All further leave was stopped.

It was in this quiet, pawky, undemanding and unimportant world that we heard in the kitchen on a Sunday morning the voice of a man who I was told was Mr Chamberlain. The war had begun, and childhood was promptly over.

CHANNEL CROSSING

DIRK BOGARDE

I N THE TRAIN from Calais to Wimereux we had the whole compartment to ourselves, which was very nice indeed. There really wasn't much room for anybody else anyway. On one side sat Lally and myself and my sister . . . that was three; and opposite, sitting in a gloomy row and looking very white and rotten, were the three Chesterfield children, Angelica, Beth and Paul, and their nanny who was called Amy O'Shea and who was older than Lally and wore a grey two-piece suit and a white straw hat with a black ribbon like a man's. She was pretty ugly too. And skinny. And sat there clutching her huge handbag as if it had all their money in it. Which it didn't. Our fathers and mothers had all that. And they were coming by motor-car to Wimereux because it was more

comfortable and in any case there wasn't room for us all in the O.M.

They were all looking so white and gloomy because they had all been terribly sick on the boat, which was really a bit funny because none of us were. And that made us feel very good. We had been to Wimereux quite often for holidays so we knew what to expect. Every time we got on the boat Lally would make us sit up on the deck and eat lemons. It wasn't a very nice thing to do but we did it because she said it stopped you being seasick, and the air was good for us.

So we did that. And we were never sick although Lally once said she felt queasy and hoped no one would speak to us because she'd have a terrible turn and what would we do then?

But this day everything had been lovely. Sunny, with a wind and the sea all glossy and pale and foamy like ginger beer; and gulls swinging over the funnels, and the flags streaming in the breeze. The Chesterfields all went down below to a cabin, which Lally told Amy was a Silly Thing To Do. And it was. Almost as soon as we left Folkestone Paul Chesterfield came up on deck with a white face and said that Amy had fallen down in a heap and had knocked her hat off.

When we got to the cabin she was sitting on the edge of a bunk holding her head, her hat all squint, and her pince-nez, hanging from her lapel by a little gold chain, were glinting in the sun.

'I'm taken bad!' she moaned. 'If only it would keep still for a minute I'd be all right, I'm sure. It's the floor swaying about so. Oh! What will become of us all if I'm taken queer?' Lally was very brisk indeed and ordered Angelica and Paul and Beth up on the deck, and told Amy to put her feet up and cover her eyes with a handkerchief.

Amy moaned and rolled from side to side and said No. No! Nothing would make her move and the children were to stay within her sight for she was Responsible. Angelica was sitting bolt upright like a white rabbit, and Beth just crouched in a corner holding on to the handle of the little door which led to the lavatory.

'Oh! Make it stop, dear God!' cried Amy, which made my sister and me giggle. Lally hit us sharply and said, 'What a silly thing to say, Miss O'Shea! If the good Lord stopped the boat now for you, we'd all be swinging about here for dear knows how long . . . soon as we get on the sooner we'll be on dry land.'

'I'll never see the land again. God help us all,' moaned Amy O'Shea and gave a dreadful gasp and covered her face with her handkerchief which smelled of lavender water. Suddenly Beth made a strangling sort of noise and Lally spun us both round and sent us up the stairs. We heard a splashing noise and then the door slammed shut.

We had a very nice time looking at all the people lying on the deck with big white enamel bowls beside them. They all looked very green and sad, only the sailors looked cheerful, and they were dashing about the sloping decks laughing and eating big ham rolls and sloshing water everywhere. We called out 'Bonjour!' to them all,

and they all waved back and said 'Bonjour' also. It was a *very* nice feeling, as if we had always been travelling which was very good for you because, as Lally said, it broadened your mind.

In a little while we could see the long flat line of land ahead . . . and the sunshine sparkling on white sailing boats and the windows of houses in France where we were going to spend four weeks at the Hôtel d'Angleterre. Lally joined us by the rail pulling on her gloves and snapping her handbag shut, she tucked a bit of hair under her hat with the ivy leaves on it, and said: 'Miss O'Shea's in a poor way, I'm afraid. They've all been sick. But what can you expect all cooped up in that little room with no air and no lemons?'

We felt sorry for them in a vague way, but quite glad about Angelica who was really so prim that a bit of seasick would do her good. Beth, who was two years younger than Angelica, was rather a nice girl and we quite liked her. She had a freckly face and gaps in her teeth but she liked doing nearly all the things we liked doing, so she wasn't a Drawback. Paul was the youngest and Not Very Well because he had something wrong with his chest which made him very pale and quiet and he spent most of his time reading. So we didn't pay any attention to him much except to say 'Good morning, Paul,' or 'Hello, Paul,' or 'Are you having a nice day?' just things like that which he only had to say 'Yes' or 'No' to, which is what he did. And nothing more.

We watched France get nearer and nearer, and heard the boat make slowing-down noises, and the water thrashing and churning about under the propellers . . . and then we could see the great clock at Calais swing into view, and all the crooked houses; and cranes striking up into the sky, like schoolteachers' fingers. The gulls wheeled and screeched and scattered over the ginger-beery water like handfuls of rice at a wedding. And the sun glinted on the slimy green seaweedy walls of the piers while men in blue rushed all alongside throwing ropes at us, shouting and whistling. It was very exciting to feel the big ship slide slowly into her place, nudging and bumping gently at the high stone walls, and watching all the ropes growing taut to stretching point as they made us fast.

Then in a flash the gangplanks were up and we all wobbled down to stand on the cobbled road of the docks. We stood there among piles of wooden boxes smelling of fish, and still felt the land swaying a little after the movement of the ship. Lally went off into the crowd of people, looking for Amy and the Chesterfields who wouldn't leave their cabin until the ship had really stopped and everything was quite still. And then they had a terrible job getting down the gangplank because it was steep and Amy's bag, Angelica's books, and the travelling rugs seemed to all get mixed up. But eventually, pale and exhausted, they were all among the fish, and we started to make our way over to the station. It took quite a while to sort out all our luggage, find the tickets, and say 'merci' to everyone in sight: Lally said we had to because you never knew who was driving the train.

In the end we all clambered into one compartment together in the middle, just in case anything hit us in the front, or from the back, and then we were assured by Lally, we'd be completely safe and not get squashed which was often the case On French Railways.

'I do think it's exciting!' said my sister happily, but no one answered her because, with a terrific shriek of the whistle and three big jig-joggy-jerks, the train started to steam out of the station into the sunlit town.

Amy O'Shea sat bolt upright looking fearfully out of the windows to see how fast we were going, and Angelica and Beth just stared ahead. Paul went to sleep.

'He's just like the Dormouse in Alice,' whispered my sister.

Lally took off her gloves and started to count all the bits of luggage on the racks, nodding her head and counting under her breath, and suddenly we roared into a tunnel and everything was black and I heard Amy O'Shea cry out in fright but we were soon through and out into the fields full of streams and little clumps of willows. There were men and women working in the fields with horses, and a girl of our age, with a flock of sheep, waved to us and we waved back like anything. Except the Chesterfields, who just sat.

from *A Postillion Struck by Lightning*

GETTING WHEELS

DAVID JACOBS

I WAS RATHER PLEASED with the bargain I had struck with Mrs Muir: not merely a wage of ten shillings a week – half-a-crown better than in my first job – but my lunch as well. My duties were to look after her ponies and help out around the farm. Alas! at the end of the week I was out of work again; Mrs Muir told me she was very sorry but she could not afford to continue employing me. I never discovered whether she couldn't afford the money (or the lunch) or whether, like my uncle and aunt, she had never expected me to stick at farm work when I discovered how hard it was.

There was a third possibility: that my work was so bad that she couldn't afford to have me wrecking her farm any longer. But this I dismissed from my mind as too defeatist and begged her to find me a job elsewhere. I told her that I would like best to be on a farm or near the horses that I loved so much, and, thanks to Mrs Muir's

kind inquiries and telephone calls, I began work the following Monday with Miss Somerville, who ran the Bell Riding Stables on the outskirts of town. Miss Somerville was in her mid-fifties, short, sinewy and grey-haired. At first meeting she seemed, like her stables, to be a little over-horsey and untidy. But as soon as she put on her riding kit she became a neat and commanding figure. She certainly knew how to command the horses and me – ruling us with a rod of iron.

The stables were very much on the outskirts of town, in fact a good three miles from the house in Bunch Lane; so the first thing I did with my one and only ten shillings from Mrs Muir was to walk into Haslemere and find a cycle shop.

It was, in fact, more than a cycle shop; it was the biggest hardware store in town and it had that indescribably stimulating smell that every ironmonger's has: a smell whose main ingredients come from wood and bright, strong, carefully-oiled, unused metal and that is at once so authoritative and so full of balm that the customers examine the goods with admiration and devotion and never a whisper of criticism and the assistants are more polite and patient and yet knowledgeable and reliable than in any other kind of business you can name. I have a theory that all ironmonger's assistants are rather saintly men and that an evil one could not stay in employment even as long as a day: the sheer solid goodness of the place would get him down and drive him out into the street frothing with rage and frustration.

It was at the far end of the shop that I found the bicycles, cradled in their own perfume, whose elements were inner-tubes, lubricating-oil, saddle-bags, rubber puncture patches and celluloid handle-grips: some standing straight and prim in racks, some rather pathetically strung up to the ceiling by their rear wheels like carcasses in a butcher's cold store, and others frankly coquettish, front-wheel tilted sideways, handlebar on hip. I chose one from the row that hung above my head: a very plain, utilitarian model. I regretted later not having thrown my bonnet over the windmill and embarked on the extra instalments that would have brought me cable brakes – but I was in no mood for wasting money on luxuries; I was there to buy the necessary equipment to get me to my new job on time and I was doing it as cheaply as possible. And let there be no suspicion that I did not prize my new acquisition. No car that I have ever bought has given me as great a thrill as that first bicycle.

Grandma signed the agreement as guarantor and promised me sixpence a week towards the cost. I rode home clutching a blue card with a surprisingly large number of spaces for recording my weekly instalments of Is. 6d. – the card somehow giving me a greater feeling of ownership than the bicycle itself. Shortly afterwards, the rear mudguard was decorated with the letters A.R.P. (M.). I had been accepted as a messenger in the Civil Defence Corps.

from *Jacobs' Ladder*

COMIC CUTS

BILL TIDY

MR HILL

LIVERPOOL MAY 1940

ALL OF THE WINDOWS IN ANFIELD ROAD SCHOOL
BROKEN DURING A NIGHT AIR RAID. NOBODY WAS
HURT, AND WE WERE ALL DELIGHTED AT THE RESULT—
AND THE GOLDMINE OF SHRAPNEL, INCENDIARY BOMB
FINS AND CANISTERS WAITING IN THE STREETS FOR US
AVID COLLECTORS AND SWAPPERS. ANY ITEM
WITH WRITING ON IT HAD DOUBLE VALUE —
AND IF IT WAS **GERMAN** YOU WOULDN'T
PART WITH IT FOR GOLD

AN AUTHENTIC
'VERDAMTE ENGLÄNDER'
EQUALS 16 PIECES OF SHELL
SHRAPNEL OR 2 SUPERMAN
COMICS. GERMAN KIT
AND UNIFORMS AS
PORTRAYED IN FILMS
AND NEWSREEL...

RAT..TAT.RAT.

... SEEMED SO MUCH BETTER AND
SMARTER THAN OURS. IN GAMES IN THE
PLAYGROUND I WAS ALWAYS AN ME.109 OR FW.190.

AMERICAN COMICS

BECAUSE OF ITS SEAGOING POPULATION AND AMERICAN SERVICEMEN STATIONED LOCALLY AMERICAN COMICS BECAME THE MAJOR JUVENILE INDUSTRY. SOME BOYS HAD MORE THAN 100 COMICS, IN COLOUR AND ON GOOD PAPER. SUPERMAN, CAPTAIN MARVEL AND BATMAN WERE THE ONLY ONES TO BE TAKEN SERIOUSLY, TORCH AND WONDERWOMAN WERE FOR WIMPS. SWAPPING WAS AN INVOLVED AND SERIOUS BUSINESS.

IN WINTER WE WOULD PUNCH HOLES IN CANS OF VARIOUS SIZES, FILL THE INSIDE WITH ANYTHING WITH A LONG BURNING LIFE, AND SWING THE THING ON A LONG WIRE HANDLE AROUND OUR HEADS.

I DON'T RECALL ANYONE EVER BEING BURNED EVEN THOUGH THE BLAZING OBJECT FLASHED THROUGH THE AIR WITH A FURNACE ROAR! THERE WERE OF COURSE A FEW SMASHED SKULLS...

FOOD WAS RATIONED, BUT EVEN THOUGH I JOINED IN, I ALWAYS THOUGHT THE PRACTICE OF SHAKING A JAR OR BOTTLE OF MILK AND SALT FOR ABOUT 4 HOURS TO PRODUCE A TINY NOB OF BUTTER WAS UTTERLY STUPID. IF ONLY WE COULD HAVE PRODUCED CHEWING GUM OR HERSHEY BARS... I REMEMBER SWEETS COMING OFF RATION. IT WAS A SUNDAY AND THE KIDS COULDN'T GET NEAR THE SHOPS FOR ADULTS!

FOOTBALL IN THE STREET

WE WERE ALWAYS TOLD TO GO AND PLAY IN THE PARK, BUT THE ROCK-LIKE BALDNESS OF STANLEY PARK WAS HARDER ON THE KNEES THAN THE PAVEMENTS OF ROBARTS ROAD, AND THE PLACEMENT OF AIR RAID SHELTERS WAS IDEAL FOR A 30-A-SIDE STREET GAME WITH A TENNIS BALL

(OBLIGATORY BRICKS AND BOTTLE ON ROOF)

WHENEVER I SEE A SOCCER LINESMAN CHECKING A 79TH. MINUTE SUBSTITUTE IT NEVER FAILS TO REMIND ME OF MY MOTHER

' HAVE YOU BEEN PLAYING FOOTBALL IN YOUR BEST (ONLY) SHOES AGAIN?'

NOSTALGIA

FOR THE RECORD

JOHN AMIS

I HAD BEEN PASSIONATE about the gramophone from a very early age indeed. I was often given as a birthday or Christmas present a toy gramophone that went 'phut' after about ten days of over-use. By that time I knew the little seven-inch records by heart and endeavoured to revive the dead gramophone by pushing the record round with one hand, sticking my fingernails in the grooves and singing the music. Eventually I was given a proper 'table-model' gramophone and I shall never forget the excitement of that first encounter, the smell of the polished wood and the packets of fibre and steel needles that went with it. We had few records at any time and all pocket money that did not go on sweets, laboriously saved up and augmented twice a year by birthday or Christmas gifts, went on records. The choice was agonizing but enthralling. Vocal gems from *Turandot*, the overture to *Die Zauberflöte*, Liszt's *Hungarian Rhapsody No 2*, which developed a recurring groove near the beginning because the cellos and double-basses in Stokowski's famous orchestral transcription went so low and deep.

I could never afford to buy more than one record at a time so that I knew parts 3 and 4 of Franck's *Variations Symphoniques* better than parts 1 and 2. (That was Alfred Cortot with a splosh of wrong notes on the last chord.) Inherited from somewhere was a single-sided disc of Rachmaninov playing Chopin's Waltz in E flat with a glamorous expanse of shiny black wax on the back. It was much thicker than a normal disc too. Certain pieces would inspire in me a sort of mental orgasm: the Franck did it in side 4 and so did a record that a grown-up friend once brought for me to hear by a composer I had never heard of called Delius. The effect that *On hearing the first cuckoo in spring* had on me was so obviously profound that the kind man, Harold Hersee, an amateur-acting friend of the family, generously gave it to me.

Life seemed to revolve round these revolving records for me. I would give my family for presents at Christmas, records that, by an amazing coincidence, I happened to want. I can remember asking my father once for the *Meistersinger* overture for my birthday. The poor man could not find it at the shop so brought me instead the intermezzos from *The Jewels of the Madonna* by Wolf-Ferrari. Mind you, I came to like those intermezzos a little later but even when I hear them today they still bring that initial feeling of tearful rage and disappointment. My father Jimmy was simply bewildered by my tears. I had been looking forward for weeks to the grand sound of the opening of Wagner's overture with its majestic tread and endless chains of harmonies refusing to come to a cadence. To be fobbed off with those wispy little Italian flute tunes and harp tinkles, quasi-archaic traceries – ugh! But soon he

found the Wagner overture and I loved him for it. Loved the record too, not just the music but even the record itself, the dark green label, the gold lettering, the magic of the name of the conductor, Leo Blech (no relation to Harry), and the difference in texture between the grooves and the shiny bit in the middle with the double-looping lines where the needle would go on and on and on until stopped.

Sometimes it was clear what I wanted to buy next but at others the choice was a pleasurable agony. Finally, when enough sixpences had been put aside – eight weeks-worth for a plum HMV or dark blue Columbia, twelve weeks-worth for the red label or light blue, the colours were magical in themselves – came the supreme moment, going to Craven's, the record shop almost opposite the Odeon in West Norwood High Street. Before taking the record home I would ask to listen to it in the showroom on a Cadillac-long radiogram which produced ten times the volume that my puny little thing at home could manage. Listening to Stokowski's record (ten-inch black label) of Debussy's *Fêtes*, not just knowing it was mine but this wonderful all-embracing sonority . . . this was indeed a supreme moment for a child that had never heard a symphony concert. Another thrill was the Fugue from *Schwanda the Bagpiper* by Weinberger, with its mounting excitement crowned by the entry of the organ full tilt and six extra trumpets in unison. Then came the panic of getting home intact the highly breakable 78 record; after which there were hours of enjoyment at home, playing the latest disc until it was almost worn out.

In the early years I always bought orchestral music but in my teens, weaned temporarily from the classics by my sister, I would buy jazz records which were cheaper than the classics. Fats Waller fascinated me, so did Art Tatum, Fred Astaire, George Gershwin's *Rhapsody in Blue*, Alec Templeton's *Bach Goes to Town*. In my later teens came the first time I bought more than one record at a time. It was Rachmaninov's Piano Concerto No 2, with Benno Moiseiwitsch as soloist and the orchestra conducted by Walter Goehr, four records, sixteen shillings. If this was the sort of book that indulged in such fancies I would

On Exmouth Sands, aged somewhere between 2 and 3

add, 'Little did I then think that one day I would meet some of the people whose names I dwelt on with such reverence – like Moiseiwitsch, for example, and Walter Goehr who I came to know quite well.'

My dream for many years was to work in a record shop, a dream which came true when I was eighteen; I spent two years of happiness amongst a whole shop full of nothing but classical music, after which I moved on to live music. But I have never lost that feeling of excitement and curiosity when faced with a stack of records. In a secondhand shop these days if I come across old 78s I cannot resist turning them over, every one, to see what is written on those magic labels.

Adapted from: *Amiscellany: My Life, My Music*

A SCHOOLBOY'S HEROES

JACK ROSENTHAL

IN THOSE DAYS, other schoolkids had heroes that you'd actually heard of – Tom Finney, Wilf Mannion, Stanley Matthews, Frank Swift, Peter Doherty, Raich Carter, Len Shackleton . . .

Where we lived, it was different. It was even a different language.

Saturday mornings, a shouted conversation with your pals across the street went something like this:

'Atta beyan deyan?' (Are you going down to Turf Moor?)

'Oor thi lakin?' (Who are their opponents?)

'Bugger oor thi lakin!' (I've no interest in their opponents!)

'Na then, then!' (Fair enough!)

And by one o'clock, we'd emerge from the railway station, run the gauntlet between (at the last count) eleven chip shops and fourteen pubs, to arrive, by twenty past, at the ground. With an hour and ten minutes to wait. Alone. And dying of exposure.

Looking back on it, the whole of the 1946–47 season seems to have been played on snowbound pitches under leaden skies. But maybe that's just looking back on it.

It was the first season of the full football programme since Hitler had stopped play back in 1939. We'd been waiting for it a long time. So now, each week, an hour and ten minutes was nothing. Especially when you were going to see what *we* were going to see.

We stood, frozen-daft, behind the goals, eating hot torpedoes. (Hot torpedoes were an East Lancashire version of Cornish pasties, a now-extinct version made of real pastry with real meat inside.) The hour and ten minutes became an hour. The hour became three quarters. Gradually, another twenty-odd thousand worshippers would come shuffling in; sucking warmed air through their scarves, blowing on their mittens, stamping their chilblained clogs. Then the last, endless fifteen minutes . . . memorising every word in the programme, every digit in the League Table, the printer's name.

And then, at last, they appeared. Our unsung, unforgettable heroes, who somehow went unnoticed by the rest of you. The Lads in Claret. Our Team. Burnley. Listen – Strong; Woodruff, Mather; Attwell, Brown and Bray; Chew, Morris, Billingham, Potts and Kippax.

Told you you've never heard of them. But read that team-list again. Read it slowly, savour the syllables – and it's poetry. Say it quickly, roll out that rhythm on your tongue – and it's a magic incantation.

All right, fair's fair, maybe the lads themselves weren't really poetry. Or magic. They were more what the *Reynolds News* called *dour*. But they were also funny, heartbreakingly unlucky and lovable. The common-or-garden Second Division lot out of which Jimmy McIlroy and Tommy Cummings were yet to flower.

Out they came. First, striding purposefully, already in an angry mood, Alan Brown, the captain. Brow furrowed, jaw set, Prometheus looking for trouble.

Behind, galloping to keep up with his strides, came the rest. Goalie Jimmy Strong, looking earnest, always earnest; little Billingham; littler Jackie Chew – and, littler still, little Billy Morris, looking up at both of them. Harold Mather like a bull-necked centurion tank. George Bray, rough, tough, elbowing the ribs and tapping the ankles of his nearest team-mate for practice. Reg Attwell, a former-day Danny Blanchflower, artistic, cultured, like Arthur Miller in his underpants. Harry Potts, blonde hair shimmering in the sun (I may have been wrong about the leaden skies), running like an athlete in training, his forearms held parallel to his shoulders. Peter Kippax with his black, Brylcreemed hair, the slightly bored, always slightly unfit wizard of the wing, harbouring inarticulately the same aspirations that George Best, sadly for us all, fully articulated a generation later. And at the back, always last, by tradition, for luck, Arthur Woodruff, bullet-jawed, a great billowing cloud of yellow hair, upright and rigid as though he had a goalpost strapped to his spine.

The Lads. Kicking in – with one ball between the eleven of them. With their short back and sides. Socks bulging with layers of shinpads, and long, flowing shorts flapping round their knees.

Heroes? Mythical kings.

They'd prepare for the kick-off, lined up against The Other Buggers. Looking back on it, The Other Buggers always seem to have played in white with black shorts. Perhaps because almost every other colour clashes with Claret and Blue. But

maybe that's just looking back on it.

They'd kick off – and for the next ninety minutes we'd suffer. Chew playing the one-two, then the three-four, then the five-six ('For God's sake, Cowboy, get rid of it!!'), then the seven-eight with Welsh International Billy Morris, till we went dizzy and Welsh International Billy Morris fell on his behind. Kippax weaving, swerving, hopscotching round his full-back, then suddenly losing interest and nodding off to sleep. Potts, careering off on long, solo runs, beating everybody, beating the goalie, then, with long-perfected precision, smacking the ball against the crossbar. Billingham (or sometimes Harrison, the alternating Number 9) buzzing round The Other Buggers' penalty-box, like a bee with B.O. . . . almost, but never quite, getting a touch of the ball.

'Everything bar score', which is in Lesson One of the Football Fan's Primer, was invented at Turf Moor in 1946–47. It was fashioned from a sigh. From twenty thousand chapped lips, under noses with dew-drops on the end, under tear-glazed eyes.

The one consolation, week in week out, was that The Other Buggers' forward-line, equally, might just as well as have stayed in the changing room playing pontoon. It needed greater mortals to as much as get a peep at Burnley's defensive wall. And most great mortals would be in Burnley Reserves.

Everyone else was left standing. By Attwell, lunging into sweeping, surf-riding, sliding tackles that seemed to cover half the width of the pitch; by Bray, irritably flicking off Other Buggers like dandruff; by Policeman Brown, guarding his penalty area like a Mother Pterodactyl – and clearing every centre at least forty yards upfield with one vicious clout of his head; by Woodruff and Mather finding touch with the classic, now-discarded, Big Boot; and finally, by earnest Jimmy Strong, loping earnestly between his posts.

Half-time, no goals. And our heroes would trundle off, shaking their heads at the injustice of life, as though even God had been brainwashed by the *Daily Herald* into believing they really were 'an unfashionable club in a small cotton town'.

Off they went, and on came another team. Instead of Claret and Blue, black raincoats with black peaked caps; and bugles instead of a ball. This, my lords, ladies and gentlemen, was the Borough Prize Band. Round the pitch they'd shuffle and plod, giving Souza what-for, kidding us into thinking we were having a good time, while we waited for the other half-time scores to go up on the notice-board. Specially those of the Second Division leaders – Manchester City, Tottenham and Birmingham.

One joyful day, the Borough Prize Band apparently turned transvestite. Running, skipping, giggling onto the pitch came what even we schoolkids could only describe as *girls*. A dozen or so young ladies carrying bugles and trombones, music stands and music. *Sheet* music. On the windiest day of the year.

For ten minutes, they tried to balance their music stands on the mud, and their

'Rosenthal of the Rovers' –
second from right, front row. Aged 17

sheet music on the music stands. And for ten minutes the wind swirled down and scattered their sheets about the pitch. Each time they gathered them up and got ready to play on the count of four, the wind did it again on the count of three.

But, if you're Music Makers to Heroes, you don't give up. And they didn't. As the teams trotted out for the second half, the wind, out of compassion or embarrassment or devilment, dropped to a whisper. And with twenty-two footballers standing about getting frostbite, the Girls Band swung into song. The ref waited, the linesmen waited, the players waited, twenty thousand bemused spectators waited, and the girls played on. And defiantly on. And only came to an end when the sheet music did. The players helped them off with their music stands and trumpets, the crowd clapped politely – if vaguely – and everyone got back to real life.

The second halves at Burnley were the same as the first. Only even more frustrating. Harry Potts, as a gesture, would hit the crossbar another six or seven times; little Billy Morris, having the shortest distance to fall, would spend more time on his behind than off; and Billingham (or Harrison) would break world records for being offside with an open goal grinning sarcastic invitation.

Then . . . yes. Being Heroes, they'd finally score. Often a two-yard trickling shove from someone's shinpad through a tangle of twenty-one players. But, nevertheless a goal. And, with it, two points.

Back to the station with our hearts singing (there was no vocal singing at football matches in those days), past the eleven chippies and fourteen pubs, and home on the train. Re-living every second of our dramatic win, savouring every shot, every pass, tackle, save, corner and throw-in. Happy that our shouted advice from the terraces hadn't been in vain – 'Boot it upfield! Give it some clog! Get rid! Thump it! Get his kneecap!' Sighing, uncomprehendingly, that all our eleven heroes weren't picked for their country.

At six-thirty on Saturday evenings, the Pink appeared. Pink being almost as emotive as Claret and Blue. The Pink being the Sports Edition of the local paper. And there, in black and pink, among 'Bob Pryde Own Goal Beats Rovers' (ie Blackburn) and 'Stanley Flounder In The Mud' (ie Accrington) would be 'Classic Clarets Do It Again!'

The Pink seemed to carry the same headlines, the same match reports and the same scores every Saturday throughout that snow-choked winter. Blackburn never quite able to cope with their opponents and their own centre-half, Accrington sinking slowly, never – to football's eternal shame – to recover, and Burnley winning by a goal or treating us to a nerve-numbing nil-nil draw.

But *some* things were changing. The Second Division League Table for a start – Burnley moving higher and higher, chasing Manchester City for promotion, the crowds growing from twenty thousand, to thirty, to forty, to fifty, the league defensive record being inexorably smashed by Our Lads, and they, themselves, for a little light relief, turning their noble gaze to the F.A. Cup.

Heroically, they annihilated First Division Aston Villa 5–1, Coventry 2–0, Luton 3–0, First Division Middlesborough 1–0, and, in the semi-final, First Division Liverpool (with the most successful attack in football, led by Billy Liddell and Albert Stubbins) 1–0.

April, 1947. Out onto Wembley's turf, they trooped. Our Lads. Those same ones we waited for every fortnight with our shining eyes and hot torpedoes. Here at the Mecca of Football, before 99,000 spectators and, for the first time in Cup Final history, television cameras. In new silk Claret and Blue shirts with the town's crest on each proud breast.

Back home, listening to the wireless (despite the TV cameras at Wembley, no one had sets in Burnley), we had one, niggling pre-match worry: Football Fate. The unwritten laws of justice and tradition that make nonsense of being a football fan. Charlton Athletic, the First Division Other Buggers privileged to be meeting us at Wembley, had been beaten by Derby County in the Final, the season before.

The Other Buggers, therefore, had an even greater right to a fairy-tale ending than we had.

No score at half-time. No score at full-time. No score till six minutes from the end of extra-time. Then, over the wireless, came a simple sentence, simple as the death sentence: 'Hurst has the ball on the right . . . he centres . . . Welsh and Brown jump . . . they've missed it . . . It goes to Duffy . . . Duffy shoots . . . Duffy's *scored*!'

Now you'll notice that 'Duffy' isn't one of the names of our heroes. Duffy was an Other Bugger. The Charlton outside-left. He'd meant to half-volley. And he toe-ended. And earnest Jimmy Strong earnestly picked the ball out of the net.

Burnley, who'd played the entire game in a state of extreme stage fright, now tried to save it, vainly, from going down in the record books as the dullest final ever. Naturally, Harry Potts promptly hammered the crossbar from twenty yards, and everyone else came within half a greying hairsbreadth from equalising. But no one did. We'd lost at Wembley, and there's no feeling quite like it.

Three schoolkids back home switched off the wireless and went out into the street to kick a tennis ball about. None of us spoke. At some point in life you have to grow up. We did it six minutes from the end of extra-time.

When I become Prime Minister or Chairman of the F.A., that's one law I'm going to change: *no* one loses at Wembley. *Both* teams win the Cup.

It's only a bit of tin anyway.

The season came hurtling to a close. We needed one point from our last two games to win promotion. Both games away from home.

Again, three schoolboys switched on the wireless for the second-half commentary of West Ham v The Heroes. One point needed. And again, a simple sentence: 'Good afternoon and welcome to Upton Park, where the half-time score is West Ham nil. . . Burnley *five*.'

Five clear goals away from home.

Mythical kings? Emperors.

With a match to spare, and a point to spare, they'd done it. Back in the First Division after seventeen years. *And* they'd been to Wembley. Nearly – so very nearly – done the double. And no one had heard of them.

Chinese (or it may be Persian) carpets are made, purposely, with one tiny flaw, one deliberate mistake. The principle being that no-one human must be perfect. So, all right, the Clarets didn't win the Cup, but they won promotion – and most important of all – the gratitude and love of three, or maybe thirty thousand, schoolkids.

The following season, much-lauded, star-shimmering Manchester United, with a great, great side, finished up in third place. And guess who, unsung and unnoticed, were in fourth place, 0.4 of a goal behind?

Na then, then.

Thanks, lads.

DINING OUT

PRUE LEITH

I WISH I COULD say that I learnt to cook at my mother's knee, but my mother detested cooking and my only maternal culinary memory is of her burning marmalade which made the house reek for days. But I did learn greed from her, for which I am grateful. Greed, or more politely put, enthusiasm for good food, is the first requirement of a cook.

Prue (right) – a lifetime of cooking ahead

My father was an enthusiast too. My earliest grown-up treat was to be taken out to dinner, *alone*, by Dad. No competing elder brother, no attention-hogging younger one. No mother for Dad to share grown-up smiles and chat with. Just me. I loved it. From him I discovered 'Chicken in the Basket', mushroom omelettes, snails in garlic butter, and Liebfraumilch. Don't smile. These were very sophisticated matters in nineteen-fifties Johannesburg. But food wasn't the only glory of these outings. We'd have an old-fashioned lovely time, me lapped about with the warmth of being thoroughly spoiled and treated as a grown-up, and Dad relaxed and happy too. Once, when I was sixteen (and I dare say looking twenty), we went to the Johannesburg Station Restaurant, the smartest place in town in those days – white cloths, obsequious waiters with white gloves and red sashes across their jackets, Edwardian fusty finery all round. As we sat down Dad noticed a business colleague, Jock Malan, dining with some friends at another table. Malan saw my father and instantly looked away, embarrassed. Dad knew at once that he thought I must be Dad's nubile popsie, floosie, fancy bit on the side. It was an opportunity not to be missed. We spent dinner holding hands and gazing into each other's eyes, hamming it up so that we thought Malan *must* realise he was being baited. But the poor man, who knew my mother well, became more and more embarrassed, not knowing where to look, unable to properly entertain his friends or to concentrate on his food, nor to keep the outrage

from his expression.

As we left the restaurant Dad led me to Malan's table: 'Jock, I don't think you know my daughter Prue, do you?' Malan was silent for a second. Then he jumped up and lunged at my laughing father, uttering unprintable curses. We'd ruined his dinner, but I thought it very good fun.

Other early gastronomic treats were less happy.

The first time I was allowed out alone with a boy to dinner – I was fifteen – was also the first time I wore lipstick. Confronted with an incomprehensible French menu, the only words that were at all familiar (and I didn't know what they meant) were 'Spaghetti à la Bolognaise'. Desperately embarrassed, I ordered that. Now, if you have never eaten spaghetti before, you don't want to do it in public, with your lipstick accompanying the sauce down your chin, and wearing a new dress, and with a real live boy opposite you. If I hadn't been so greedy I could have just pretended I didn't like it and stopped. But I kept trying to get the things on the fork until the waiter completed my humiliation by showing me how to twirl the spaghetti into a ball by twisting the fork.

My other early gastronomic memories are equally bizarre. Both my parents had a passion for raw onion sandwiches. I remember encountering my mother making them in the middle of the night. I have inherited the desire for dead-of-night onion butties, but indulging it is vetoed by my family. I also remember sharing a room with my mother once, and just as I was dropping off she said, 'The thing that is so marvellous about *escargots* is not the snails, it's the garlicky butter, and sopping it up with bread.' Sleepy though I was, my mouth started to water and pretty soon we were both sitting up in bed, excitedly discussing the pleasure to be had from digging the snails out with a pin, and the tender resilience (rather than downright rubberiness) of the perfect snail. That edition of pillow talk ended with onion sandwiches if I remember right. Talking about food is a great appetiser.

One more treasured memory, and one to give heart to all the greedy:

When I was nine we left England for Cape Town on a Union Castle steamer. Churchill was on board, heading for Madeira. In the Bay of Biscay rough weather kept Mrs Churchill, most of my family and the entire passenger list confined to their cabins with seasickness. My brother James (age 3) and I were the only takers for fried eggs and bacon. Then Churchill joined us. James, very polite, suddenly said, 'Excuse me, Sir,' walked solemnly to a potted palm, threw up into its container, and exited.

But Churchill and I, undefeated, soldiered on to the toast and marmalade.

FIRST DATE

JAMES HERRIOT

King of the Road

IT WAS JUST after my fourteenth birthday that I became aware of a serious deficiency in my life. I had never taken a girl out.

It would never have occurred to me but for the fact that my friends at school kept discussing their love lives. Nonchalant, throwaway lines about where they had been with their female companions the night before began to puzzle and irritate me. It was an unknown world. What was wrong with me?

Fourteen-year-olds are a lot more grown-up now than they were fifty years ago, but still, I decided it was time I did something about the situation. I knew a girl who, I felt, would be suitable to help me to launch myself into this desirable life; a sweet little thing I had met on holiday on the Isle of Arran, a year younger than myself and very pretty, and I had her address, somewhere on the south side of Glasgow. I would take her to the pictures.

When she replied, accepting my invitation to see *Hell's Angels* at the Tivoli on the following Saturday, I felt a great sense of relief. I had taken the first step. From now on I would be able to join in those men-of-the-world talks at school.

I had arranged to meet her on the corner of Sauchiehall Street and Renfield Street and, as I lived at the other end of the big city, I left my home in good time on the Saturday. I had a half crown in my pocket which, I felt, would be ample for my needs – two shilling tickets, a penny each way on the tramcar and a bit left over.

I was quietly confident as I boarded the tram and asked the conductor for a penny fare.

He glared balefully at the half crown in my hand.

'Have ye no' anythin' smaller?' he barked.

'No . . . no . . .' I quavered, realising I had made a serious mistake in my planning. The Glasgow tram conductors didn't like being offered large denomination coins for small fares, and this one seemed to take it as a personal affront.

He was obviously bent on revenge, too. Grumbling and muttering about 'stupid weans', he began to dredge through his leather bag.

'C'mon, pit oot yer haund,' he grunted, then methodically counted out my change entirely in halfpennies. I needed two hands to accommodate the flow of coppers, thirty-four in all, and as the man left me he threw me a savagely triumphant glance. It had taken him quite a long time to ransack his bag for the halfpennies, but he seemed satisfied.

As soon as I stepped off the tram I saw my little partner, right on the corner as arranged, but as I chinked and jingled my way over to her, my confidence evaporated. It didn't help that she looked apprehensive as though she had never done this before, and as we made our way to the Tivoli conversation was difficult.

Those were the great days of the cinema. Everybody went to the pictures half a century ago, and a long queue stretched out onto the street. As we shuffled towards the entrance it became clear that the main film would be starting soon and at the pay box people were putting their money down quickly, grabbing their tickets and hurrying inside. That was until I arrived.

The young woman behind the glass gaped at me as I scooped my handfuls of change through the opening.

'God help us, whit's this?' she burst out as some of the halfpennies rolled into her lap and others onto the floor. She herself was under stress with the imminent start of the film and I was something she just didn't need.

It took a long time for her to collect all the coppers and for me to chase some of the errant coins across the foyer, and the queue members, with typical Glaswegian forthrightness, were not slow in voicing their displeasure.

'C'mon, get movin'!', 'What's the hold up?' were just some of the remarks, but the one which cut deepest came from an old lady.

'Puir wee soul,' she murmured.

Throughout my agony my little companion stayed close by me, and it made it worse when I saw her expression of wonderment. When we finally reached the darkness of the theatre, I felt drained.

I didn't see much of *Hell's Angels*. I had thought the whole thing was going to be so easy with lots of urbane comportment and light badinage on my part, but I sat there in silence, bathed in misery and shame.

It was another four years before I found the courage to take a girl out again.

THE FROGOLOGIST

BRIAN PATTEN

A<small>S A CHILD</small> I hated being asked what I wanted to be when I grew up (I had absolutely no idea). There were much more important things to consider, such as where about on the railway embankments I could find the best ponds for frog-spawn . . .

> I hate it when groan-ups say,
> 'What do you want to be?'
> I hate the way they stand up there
> And talk down to me.
>
> I say:
> 'I want to be a frogologist
> And study the lives of frogs,
> I want to know their habitat
> And crawl about in bogs,
> I want to learn to croak and jump
> And catch flies with my tongue,
> And will they please excuse me 'cause
> Frogologists start quite young.'

A CHILD'S VIEW OF HEAVEN

JILLY COOPER

IT SADDENS ME that I have no religion. I was an intensely devout little girl. Every morning I rushed to the mirror hoping I'd sprung a halo overnight like the Cookeen ads. Every night I spent hours praying for every individual cat, dog, pony and hen that I knew. I even enjoyed church and complained bitterly when I was taken out before the sermon.

I thought continually about my Guardian Angel. What sex was he? How was he constructed? In the end I decided he was sexless and went straight round underneath like a Teddy bear.

Religion walked in the family of course. My grandfather was a canon and I always pestered my mother for anecdotes of vicarage life when she was a child; how the bishop buttered his table mat instead of his bread when he came to lunch, how a bucket of water intended for a stray dog drenched the curate, how my aunt secretly added the cat's and dog's names to my grandmother's prayer list, so the entire Mother's Union were exhorted to pray for the return to health of Mewkins and Raggety Bones.

I think I began to go off religion when I went to kindergarten. I played the Ass in a nativity play and had to sing a song about:

Standing knee high in the straw,
Makes me love the baby more.

I was supposed to make my entrance after the Ox had mooed his bit. Unfortunately I caught sight of my mother in the audience, shrieked with joy, and completely missed my cue. Afterwards I was sharply reprimanded by the headmistress. 'You spoilt our play,' chorused the other little girls.

It's like the one about a small boy who started off playing Joseph and was demoted to the Innkeeper because he was so naughty. All went well on the day until Mary and Joseph rolled up at the Inn and asked if there were any room: 'Masses of room for everyone,' said the Innkeeper blandly. 'Come in at once.'

I might have retained a remnant of faith if religion hadn't been so rammed down my gullet at boarding school. Not only did we have to go to services twice a day, and three times on Sunday, but it was also extremely high church. Brought up

on matins, I was appalled by the incense, the bells, the genuflecting and crossing, the weedy acolytes dressed in laundry bags, the sing-song chant of the priest, and what seemed to me endless tippling of wine. I caused a furore by refusing to kneel down in Creed. But, threatened with expulsion, I naturally capitulated. I was not the stuff of martyrs.

Later I took my revenge. We had a large imposing house mistress called Miss Body. One evening I and three cronies, draped in sheets, with dressing-gown cords round our waists, staged a protest march through the dormitories. The leader bore a cross made of precariously roped-together rulers. She was followed by two acolytes swinging Morny's French Fern in place of censers. I brought up the rear (pillows tied under my sheet to resemble the vicar's paunch).

'This is Miss Body, who is given for thee,' I chanted.

'It is meet and right so to do,' sang the others, stuffing handkerchiefs into their mouths to muffle their giggles.

We were just beginning to swing when we rounded the corner, slap into the house mistress herself. Great was her wrath. She couldn't expel all four of us, however, as it would have deprived the school of an income of £1,400 a year. Instead all treats were suspended to the end of term.

The fight went out of me after that. I dispelled the tedium of those everlasting sermons by exploring the prayer book, learning about the churching of women, and the numerous kith I couldn't marry, like my husband's sister's son, and reading the prayers for famine and dearth (we never thought we got enough to eat at school).

Ironically though, it was at my confirmation that I finally parted company with religion. The build-up was so fantastic: a whole year of intensive instruction, hours of meditation alone in one's cubicle, flowers, hundreds of confirmation cards, the nunlike fervour of the other candidates.

I was going through a spotty stage at the time. And in preceding weeks, I bargained endlessly with God: 'Make me spotless of face on the day, and I promise to be spotless of sin.'

Confirmation day dawned, I had more spots than ever. Dressed in a white dress and veil of disfiguring ugliness, like something someone's Nanny left out in the rain, I stumped up the aisle to receive the bishop's sign – a vision of angels, a still small voice. Nothing happened – not the flicker of a flaming sword. Anti-climax was inevitable. I never took religion seriously again. The only thing that bothered me next morning, when I took my first communion, was composing my face in a suitably pious expression when I walked back to my seat.

from *Jolly Super*

FRENCH LESSONS

ROY HATTERSLEY

FOR MOST OF the war, I was more frightened by the French than by the Germans. French was taught at Hillsborough High School as part of the standard curriculum – one of the minor items on the *table d'hôte* menu which obscured the general low quality of the cuisine and the inadequacy of the *à la carte* alternative. It was taught to everyone in the school except the kindergarten – which, to her credit, Headmistress Bertha Roberts (Member of the Royal College of Preceptors) did not rename the nursery after the blitz. So I opened my attack on the language of Balzac, Lamartine and Molière at the age of nine – a year later than more fortunate pupils who had not been held back by asthma-enforced absence. The assault was led by Mme Wurtier, a refugee from previous hostilities against the Germans, whose minimal command of the English language (by which she had been surrounded since the occupation of Belgium in 1914) did nothing to inspire confidence in either her linguistic abilities or the essential simplicity of learning to speak a different tongue.

Like other members of the Hillsborough High School staff, Mme Wurtier was part-time to the point of absenteeism. Her place in the curriculum was justified by a confrontation with the entire 'upper school' in 'Miss Roberts's classroom' each Friday afternoon. She brought with her a pile of cards, which depicted everyday life in France. Beneath each picture was printed a juxtaposition of letters which, to me at least, was beyond comprehension. Indeed they were so unnaturally arranged that I could not properly focus my eyes upon them. Mme Wurtier dealt out her visual aids like a dealer in a poker school, sometimes palming one from the bottom of the pack in an attempt to set a sixteen-year-old girl a more difficult test of pronunciation than that which she imposed on a seven-year-old boy. I was the dunce of the class and always got *wagon lit* – which, for two years, I believed to derive its name from an integral lighting system which distinguished it from other Paris tramcars. With our cards on the desks before us, we took turns to make gargling noises based on the title of our picture. Each of us then held up for general recognition the picture which we had been allocated, and imitated, with our fellow linguists, the gargling noises made by our teacher as she obsessively checked her watch to see how much more of our company she was obliged to endure.

The seventy minutes of the double lesson was the most bewildering time of the week. The three minutes which preceded them were one hundred and eighty seconds of pure terror. Mme Wurtier was always late. Miss Roberts always left the previous lesson at the moment that the time for its appointed end was reached. Invariably, we

were 'put on our honour' not to speak a word during the transition. Invariably, everyone (except me) shouted and screamed until the classic, black-swathed figure of a Belgian widow swept through the door. My silence was the product neither of instinctive obedience nor natural taciturnity. I was so frightened that my vocal chords atrophied. For I knew the terrible retribution which would follow the discovery of our awful crime. The punishment involved what is still, for me, the most terrible torture of all – uncertainty.

Mme Wurtier did not punish us herself. Our behaviour was reported to Miss Roberts when she returned at four o'clock – in theory for the final dismissal of the week. Her reaction never varied. First of all we were harangued for our failure to keep a promise that we had never made. Driven on by desperation, I often had an insane desire to rise in my desk and argue that since we were not willing parties to the broken compact, the punishment should be reduced. But, I always shrank from the ultimate lunacy of expecting Miss Roberts to be reasonable. Instead, I sank back amongst the other miscreants and waited the next inevitable stage in the ritual drama. Each week we were invited to confess our disobedience. When no guilty hands were raised, the path of honour was abandoned and an invitation was offered to those who had remained obediently silent to indicate their virtuous record and turn Headmistress' evidence on the real culprits. All eyes were turned on me. But I never grassed. By then I was immobilised by the prospect of the horror ahead. We would be 'kept in' – but not 'kept in' for a prescribed fifteen minutes or specific half hour. We would be detained at Miss Roberts's pleasure.

And we were kept there in the upstairs room, without the comforting presence of Miss Roberts herself. Perhaps more composed children welcomed the absence of their tormentor. But to me the sight of her sitting, erect and disapproving, behind her desk would have been immensely reassuring. It would have prevented the renewed talking that inevitably broke out the moment she left, the angry expressions of anguished outrage when she returned and found us in a blatant conversation and the prolonged detention that was the invariable outcome of the other offences being taken into consideration. More important, as long as Miss Roberts was there, looking at her errant pupils, I was confident that we had not been forgotten. Without her, I grew increasingly certain that she would never return to release us, and that our lifeless bodies would be discovered by a search-party of parents long after the weekend was over.

Sometimes I tried to escape – pretending, when I was caught on the stairs, that I was on my urgent way to the lavatory. When Mme Wurtier increased her workload to two part-afternoons a week my nerve totally broke. On the day her extra duties began, I set off for school as usual but, once around the corner of Airedale Road, I doubled back into Wadsley Churchyard. It was a dark damp morning and I shuffled along the paths that divided church and vicarage, water-butt and faded-flower dump, kicking the wet leaves into which I sank up to my ankles. It was a huge

churchyard and it offered a nine-year-old with an active imagination unlimited opportunities for fantasy. The following year the cemetery was to become a battlefield in which I led an irregular army. But throughout my days of 'truancy' (as my mother always woundingly called it after my apprehension) I dreamed more peaceful dreams. During the two days which I spent amongst the laurels and cypresses, I determined to write a standard work on the English tombstone. I found a memorial to a local cricketer into which bat, ball and stumps had been carved and a headstone engraved in the pattern of blacksmith's tools that marked the last resting place of a farrier who had served with Kitchener at Omdurman. A single tomb yclept a whole family that had perished together in the great flood when the dams above Sheffield burst and the water swept through the northern valleys of the city like a tidal wave. Interred within it was 'an infant of about one year'. I was fascinated by the melancholy mystery of the churchyard, but I accepted the book in which its mortal remains were immortalised would have to omit all references to military memorials and interment of paupers. The little patch of war graves to the south of the church with its stone tablets (identical apart from the regimental badges that they wore like medals) was far too near the road for prolonged investigation by anyone who needed to keep his whereabouts a secret. And the rough acre of unloved and uncut twitch grass that covered the last unmarked resting place of the Victorian inmates of the Wadsley Asylum was too open a piece of country to be crossed by a man on the run.

I remained a fugitive from Miss Roberts's justice for almost two days. Then half way through the second afternoon my mother appeared and gently led me home. I was astonished to discover that she was more worried about the anguish which she assumed had provoked the complicated deception than she was about the truancy itself.

from *A Yorkshire Boyhood*

SAMPLES

CLEO LAINE

Pony-trekking at Margate, 1931

EVERY CHILD HAS one – a friend they adore but the parents dislike, for either snobbish reasons (ie they do not talk correctly, or they don't come from the right part of town or school, etc) or just that they're a bad influence all round, getting you to do all the things you want to do, that you know your parents will disapprove of. Well, I had one of these. He covered both categories. He talked sloppily and he was a villain in my parents' eyes. But to me and my brother he was the one we could get to do all the things our other friends wouldn't dream of doing, and we wickedly blamed him if we got caught.

Two incidents come to mind – the first, 'Bunking into the Cinema'. I don't know if it still happens, but it was a childish practice of ours. Samples (the name of our friend) would squeeze through the local cinema's toilet window and let us in at the exit door. This became such a well-known weekly adventure that not only us kids but old-age pensioners who couldn't (at that time) afford the cinema also waited for Samples to appear. Sadly his Robin Hood deed was discovered eventually and he was ejected by the powers that be, while the aged and we, his good friends, remained to enjoy the film. He never seemed to take offence – it was just great fun. And he would think up something bigger and better the next week.

The other adventure concerned the 'Rafts' – in retrospect a dangerous place to play. It was a pit that was disused and full of water, with planks of wood lying about that we used as rafts, hence the name of the place. With long poles we punted about on this abandoned lake-like patch of water, acting out a fantasy Tom Sawyer world. One day Samples thought he'd add some spice to the playing and became determined to upset our rafts and us into the water. But he miscalculated, and splashed in himself. We thought this was great fun and made him suffer a bit, as he couldn't swim, before we rescued him and got him home to our house (because his father was very strict and would have given him a beating) to dry him off in front of the fire. We didn't expect our parents, but we heard a key in the door and my father calling out, 'Is that you, Alec and Clemmie?' 'Yes, Dad,' we replied, meanwhile stuffing our disliked (by our father) friend behind the sofa just in time to be out of

view as he entered the room. We thought we had got away with it, but in trying to dry Samples out we had put him close to the fire with all his clothes on, so he was steaming by the time my dad arrived home. I guess he was suspicious of the way we were acting, and looked around the room. Seeing steam coming from the sofa he yelled, 'Is that you, Samples?' The game was up. We all got a hefty lecture. Samples was sent home damp – with a never-to-darken-the-door-again warning.

But Dad always knew when we had broken the rule – by the number of aitches we dropped when we talked!

A Night To Remember

NICHOLAS PARSONS

THE WAR WAS on. I was completing my education in Glasgow. My parents were living in London, where my father worked as a doctor, and during a break I returned home to stay with them, even though the blitz was at its height. To those who are frightened to visit London because one terrorist bomb has gone off, it must seem strange that someone should visit a city which was being bombed from the air regularly every night. This was the war, however, and attitudes are different in times of extreme peril. You become inured to a dangerous situation and fatalistic about it, which is difficult to explain to someone who has not been through the experience. Certainly this was my attitude. You went about your everyday life as best you could, and at that time in London your evenings were confined to shelters at the end of the garden or in the Underground – or, as with our family, sleeping together under a steel Morrison table in the centre of the house on the ground floor, which was considered to be the most secure place in the house other than from a direct hit.

On this evening the sirens had gone as usual around dusk. A dreaded noise that never failed to send a chill right through you, even though you had heard it many times before. You tried to be nonchalant, and keep up your spirits. Soon a distant drone of planes would be heard, then the reassuring ack-ack barrage started up, as much to keep the planes from pinpointing their target as the hope of making a direct hit. Then the *crunch-crunch* as somewhere in the distance that frightening onslaught from the skies rained down. They used to say that it was the aeroplane you couldn't hear that carried the bomb which was going to drop on or near you.

On this particular evening, however, there seemed to be a lack of that dreaded

crunch noise. It didn't seem like a normal raid. In the darkness, because of the blackout, I pulled back the curtain to look out. The sky had a kind of red glow in the distance, and there was more light than there had been at dusk. I decided to go out and investigate. It was possible to see quite clearly across the street. This was normally impossible at 9pm with the blackout, and no moon. I returned and told my father. He came out to see what I was describing, and was equally mystified. He suggested we might walk up to Hampstead Heath, which was only about half a mile from where we lived in Finchley Road, to investigate. The lack of noise from falling bombs was in itself a mystery, and as we walked in silence, lost in our own thoughts, I swear the sky grew even lighter.

We eventually arrived at the Whitestone Pond, the highest point on the Heath, and from where on a very clear day you can just make out the outline of the City of London. There was already a small group of people there, drawn by the same unusual circumstances that had attracted us. We all stared in amazement and disbelief towards the City. It was possible to see it quite clearly. It was illuminated by innumerable fires, which gave off an incandescent glow, and the intensity of those fires was turning night back into day for many miles around. The City of London looked as if it was all ablaze, a vast red and yellow fireball, as the flames leapt high into the sky. One knew it was the City because right in the centre could be seen St Paul's Cathedral, illuminated as no floodlighting could possibly achieve. It was an eerie sight. Only now do we know that this was the famous fire blitz, which was intended to destroy the heart of London by fire through the dropping of an incredible number of incendiary bombs.

My father and I stood in silence, too shocked, too disturbed to speak. Eventually I managed to say, 'Dad, what does it mean?' My father, normally rather a matter of fact man of a few words, paused, then replied with obvious emotion: 'I don't know. Whatever it is, it is pretty serious. Let's go, before we see St Paul's crumble before our eyes.' We walked back in silence. Was this the beginning of the end? How could any city survive such an onslaught? As it turned out it was more like the end of the beginning. St Paul's survived, London survived, we survived, and the rest is history.

Next morning we went up to the City to see what help we could give, and with many others handed out tea and other hot drinks to the weary firemen who were still fighting the remains of many fires. I saw at firsthand some of the most ghastly devastation it has been my experience to witness, and alone, surrounded by gutted buildings, ruined churches and rubble strewn streets, stood St Paul's, majestic and almost unscathed. I shall never forget it, but in quite a different way I shall never ever forget the sight and the experience of the previous evening.

THIRTY-SEVEN YEARS ON

TERRY JONES (AGED 44)

WRITING IS ONE of the most important things in my life, and when I look back on my childhood, I realise it always has been. Perhaps my mother knew this, and that is why she preserved a few little scraps of paper on which I had written my first school essays.

Reading these scraps now is a curious experience – here I am, aged forty-four, being button-holed across the intervening years by the rather garrulous seven-year-old me. I am not altogether sure that I like what I find, but I am grateful to my mother for preserving something of my childhood that would otherwise be impossible to retrieve – me as a child.

WHEN I GROW UP

by Terry Jones (aged 7)

Ever since I was five I'v wanted to be an actor (I'm sure of it,) or some times I think of being an muscian. Schubert came from Austria. He came to England and wrote the song the roses shine above the garden gate. Beethoven said it was the unvinished sinvone. But I'm satacvied on acting, (much better than all the two things (I mean the two I was talking about). I'll tell you my future, First I intend to have a big big house, and have a bow tie, and a black long tailed jacket and black and grey striped trousers for best when I intend to go dancing and I shall have a boler hat a top hat and a ordinery hat and jackets like my father and a rain coat (of course). But I'm not looking forward to training or Service. Personally I hope there wont be any service but I expect there will but I neednt worry because I'm too yung to worry about future. When I'm 14teen is the time to worry about life or business but really I'v got to now wile I'm yung and got the chanc. Nows the time to worry about business but I really mint Servises is'nt it now wile I'm yung, because I'm seven arnt I.

· SATURDAYS ·

by Terry Jones (aged 7)

On Saturdays it's in Winter it's generally fogy and cold but that doesnt worry Buster, a big or should I say Huge ginger haired boy, from coming round and playing football in the big field at the back of the house. it's mudy I dare say, and theres a brook at the end of the fieldf, and when the goaly kicks out, once or twice he kicks the ball in splash. The goal is two posts stuck up in the mud. We are usaly glad to get in and have tea and watch childrens hour on television (Muffin the mule. The childrens favourite announcer is Jenefer she is nine. Afterwards we makeup ghosts (Nigel is scared stiff) I wonder why, it is peculiar, Buster and I arent, and yet Buster is two years older than Nigel and I'm three years yonger than him isn't it funny. Some times we play cards or Monopoly no just a minute I mean table soccer. Buster likes that best of all. I don't. I like Monopoly best, just you try it's smashing just try. But we could go to bed later and stay up and se television. I'm hoping Hazel will come to tea with me one Sunday but on Christmus I will send her a Christmas card. I did in the infants. I am going to infite Hazal to my birthday party. I will ask a few more school frends of mine. I wonder how many I will have.

After Saturday or Sunday it feels a shame to go back to school again and when you look back on sunday and saturday it seems a long time, but I look forward to getting back to school and meeting Hazal.

Sand castles at Colwyn Bay

· MY FAMILY ·

by Terry Jones (aged 7)

We have five in our family, but we have four without granny. Granny is a Newns and our family is the Jones family. Granny is mummy's mother. Daddy is the head of the family so I will begin with him. Daddy is in the Bank and that caused him to get lodgers, (we had six). Daddy is very dark and has a very strange and prickaly mustash and has a tremendous wave on his head but he wears a hat, it is green with a feather in it. Now I will talk about mummy. Mummy is much heavyer than daddy she weighs ten stone and daddy weighs eght stone but daddy has an ulser and is not to well and it is natural he should weigh more. He has had two x-rays already and had an pipe pushed down his throat and sat like that for two hours. Mummy is a bit lighter than me. She has a little bit more hair than Mrs Ward and does not wear shoes with laces. La la (granny) is sixty-one not been well lately and has been in bed. She also has a little more hair than Mrs Ward and it is grey. She hardly ever goes out to the shops. She has Hazel eyes and is always buying us things. She considers her self quite old but she makes it too old. Nigel is fair with blue eyes and has a grey suit. On Sundays he wears blue. He is not very good at Arithmatic he goes to quier. Myself, I am not tall I am quite dark. I am a Briton and Nigel is a saxon. I like the Britons best. I am proud of Wales. I think it is the best country in the world. It is sad to look back on the old days in Wales. You ort to go there. I think six is too much for a family I think four is enough five is as much as six. But when you have two out of the way it is all right. Now I will talk about myself. I am seven and I live in Claygate Surrey. The road which I live in is riyth road. My school is Esher. I live a mile away from Esher and luckily I can ride on the bus to my school but when I am late that is often, it isn't the bus to blame it is cos it is very hard to get up erly. I lern the pino I can play quite well for my age. I am hopping to be an actor I simply love acting it is Wizard like the Wizard of Oz. Now although I am talking about my family I ort to be talking about papers. You know it must be funny to start live if you know what I mean when your about to start your first day at work it must be funny mustnt it.

A WHIFF OF THE PAST

LORD SOPER

At school at Swaffield Road, Wandsworth, 1913. Soper D. is in the centre of the front row

WRIGHT'S COAL TAR Soap is an excellent cleaning agent, but for me it is very much more than that. It is a magic carpet which transports me to the land of my childhood or, more particularly, to its holidays. Wave a bar of this soap in front of my nose and I am immediately reliving holiday experiences from more than seventy years ago. A whiff of it and memories come flooding in.

At the beginning of August in those far off days the Soper family took itself by train to Minehead. When we arrived at the boarding-house my mother understandably thought that we needed cleaning up a bit. Out came a bar of Wright's Coal Tar Soap, and the world of my childhood still floods back whenever I catch its nostalgic aroma with an immediacy which is Proustian but much more simple.

Usually we travelled down to Somerset on the first Saturday in August and, believe it or not, the very first excursion we made was not down to the sea but to discover the whereabouts of the Methodist Church. If we were to begin our holiday properly on the first day, which was also the first day of the week, then Sunday observance came before holiday activities. Such was the quality and aroma of those holidays, renewed and as vital now as they were then. Though perhaps I ought to

add that the strict Sabbatarian discipline which would not allow us to go bathing on Sunday no longer carries the same absolute requirements as it did then.

In one sense the holiday began on the Monday. The unpacking of the trunk had begun on the Saturday night. For most of the year this tin box played no part in my life, but about a fortnight before the holiday began it appeared in our front room at home and the ceremony of filling it began. Each of us three children was allowed to contribute, but not too much. Nevertheless it still amazes me as to what in fact found its way into that trunk. When full to bursting, it was roped up and a card was put in the front window inviting Carter Paterson to take it to Minehead. It always seemed a little short of miraculous that when we arrived there the trunk had preceded us and was sitting in our diggings.

Then down to the beach complete with what was quite correctly called a collapsible tent. This structure was composed of a number of parts and my father was responsible for assembling them. We were enrolled as assistants and all the more enthusiastic to see it erected, because only then could we get into our bathing costumes and test the water. The assembly of the tent was by no means easy. My father was indomitable. I once remember him saying that he'd get that wretched tent up if it was the last thing he did! Which even now has an almost apocalyptic ring to it. We took it in turns to undress inside it and thence into the sea – *en famille*.

It was all great fun and I especially remember the difficulties we had with one of my aunts who often came with us on holiday. There was something wrong with her centre of balance. She could swim quite well, but when endeavouring to stand up again in the water her head went down and her feet went up! I don't know what would have happened if we hadn't been on hand to up-end her from time to time.

If swimming and basking in the sun (and it seemed to shine most of the time in those far off days) and playing ball games filled most of the day, the high spot of the evening was the bandstand where Uncle Mac's concert party presided. Its initial attraction was that you did not have to pay to go in – it was a free for all out of doors and I found it irresistible. I wonder how many who may read these words remember 'The pretty little girl from Nowhere' which was one of Uncle Mac's most popular hits. My father recollected the words, my brother, my sister and I reproduced the tune and we played it and sang it on the boarding-house piano, whereafter it became part of our musical repertoire at home. I daresay it infringed copyright but it was a constant and happy reminder of the concert party and its genuine delights.

Those were the days that the whiff of a bar of soap revitalises so long after they happened, and with an immediacy which destroys the passage of time. 'Time like an ever rolling stream,' says the hymn, 'bears all its sons away.' This is true inasmuch as we are mortal beings and our earthly span is strictly limited, but when the hymn goes on to assert that we, or our years, 'fly forgotten as a dream dies at the opening day' – I beg to differ. A simple sense, such as the sense of smell, can preserve and so re-enact the past and enable us mortals to enjoy something of eternity.

A CURIOUS CHARACTER

CHRISTINA FOYLE

IT IS A great good fortune to be born a bookseller's daughter – to have every book in the world to read, to meet writers, artists, people from all over the world. All my life my favourite haunt has been Foyles, our bookshop in the Charing Cross Road, with its stock of six million volumes.

I used to spend all my spare time there when I was a child and my favourite place was the Occult Department, where we kept books on Spiritualism, Black Magic, the Tarot cards, and everything that was weird and wonderful.

However, for me, the principal attraction was the man in charge, Mr Hillary George. Tall, extremely good looking, with wavy golden hair and a delightful smile, he held court daily among the numerous middle-aged ladies who called to seek books on Spiritualism and the inner light.

Christina Foyle (middle) shouldering arms

Although he was so sought after, Hillary George always had time for me. He had a tiny office behind the bookshelves and there he would produce the loveliest children's books and read them to me – Andrew Lang, Kipling, Stevenson – books illustrated by Edmund Dulac and Arthur Rackham. It was through him that I discovered the joy of books.

Often he would take me to lunch in a Soho restaurant and it was with him that I first tasted ravioli and zabaglioni. Books, delicious food, exquisite company, they were days of enchantment.

And then, catastrophe! I went to Foyles, to the Occult Department as usual, and he was not there – he had gone. I was devastated. My father told me the reason.

In those days there was a weekly periodical called *John Bull* which specialised in exposing charlatans – like Horatio Bottomley, its first editor. This paper had published a sensational article on my friend, describing how he

exploited the ladies who came to him for spiritual books and guidance, and described the large sums of money that had come his way from these trusting people he was helping towards the inner light.

I was heartbroken that he had gone, and the Occult Department lost all attraction for me, especially as his place was taken by a retired clergyman who was led astray by the arch-magician, Aleister Crowley. But that is another story.

Then I saw him again. One day, as a special treat, my father took me to lunch at the Savoy. At a table nearby, immaculately dressed, as attractive as ever and accompanied by three middle-aged ladies, was Hillary George.

He came over to greet us and I told him how much I missed him and thought of him. He said, 'You must not worry. Since that article appeared in *John Bull* I have never looked back. Every post brings more seekers after enlightenment. My life is full and complete.'

I was pleased that for my friend, Hillary George, it was a happy ending.

A LOOK BACK TO THE TWENTIES

PATRICK MOORE

SINCE I WAS born in 1923, looking back to my boyhood is rather a long time ago. It was a different sort of world then. We were still a united nation; law and order was maintained; it was safe to walk around alone. In fact my own boyhood was punctuated by illness – I managed two terms at prep school without being away much, and subsequently I passed Common Entrance, but it was not until I was sixteen that I was really able to act in the same way as everyone else. By then the war was starting and I manoeuvred my way into the R.A.F. as a flyer. But to hark back to those early days at prep school . . .

I have always had a major handicap – I am, without the shadow of a doubt, the clumsiest person in three continents. If I try to screw two bits of wood together, the screw goes crooked and I have to hammer it, with disastrous results. If I try to replace an electric light bulb, it promptly falls out. I was the same even in my early days, and I remember that I unwittingly drove two people demented. Both were masters at the prep school. One of them was the woodwork master, whose name,

Stargazer and friend

believe it or not, was Mr Wood. We only had his class once a week, but at the start of term all of us were asked what we wanted to make, and under supervision we set to work. The class numbered about a dozen, I suppose, with an average age of ten.

The other boys decided to make the usual kinds of things – picture frames, shelves, wall-racks and so on. My ambition was to make a boat. Mr Wood must have known that this was courting disaster, but he provided me with a large chunk of wood, a hammer, a chisel, a rag, and told me to begin by hollowing out the hull.

This sounded easy, even for me, and I started in brimful of confidence. By the second or third class I had shaved away about a third of the block, not very tidily, but well enough. Two-thirds of the way through the term, when the other boys were nearly finished, I was down to the last stages of making the hull. Calamity followed. During the last three classes I put the chisel through the bottom so many times that the whole project had to be abandoned. It was my first and last attempt; I doubt if Mr Wood was ever quite the same again.

The other episode occurred slightly earlier, and involved Art. I admit that I am totally art-blind. If I see a superb picture in a wonderful frame, hanging in a majestic gallery, I tend to look for the joke underneath. School art classes were not very serious, and again about weekly, but occasionally we had Drawing Prep and on one occasion we were told to draw a towel hanging over a chair. I misheard and for some strange reason I gathered that I was to draw a *cow* hanging over a chair. I did my best, and at the next class I produced it. The art master took one look, gave a strangled gulp, and asked me what it was. When I told him he had the grace to believe me; but he then wrote to my parents and pointed out that although I was very keen and it was nice to have me in the class, there wasn't really a great deal of point – and it would surely be better for all concerned if during future art classes I went off into the music-room and played the piano quietly to myself.

I did – and that ended my art career.

I do also remember one of the very few glorious occasions when I was fit enough to play cricket. I was given the ball and told to bowl. As I loped up to the stumps I gripped the ball hard, and instinctively realised that I could spin it. It hit the

batsman's middle stump – the first leg-break I ever bowled, though how many thousands I have delivered since then I wouldn't like to say. That was a great moment; not until I was in the R.A.F. did I begin to play seriously, but that first wicket is engraved in my memory. At least it was more successful than my art or woodwork, at which, I regret to say, I have never made any progress, and fear that I will never do so now!

BIRDIE

LIBBY PURVES

T HERE WERE FOUR of us children, and we had a restless and wandering sort of childhood. My father was in the Foreign Service, and once every two or three years would come that exciting and frightening moment when he came home with a certain expression on his face and said he had news for us. News meant a posting, and it could be almost anywhere. As often as not, it caused a certain amount of confusion: I remember excitedly looking at South America on the globe when we were in fact heading for South Africa. Sometimes it caused major disruption to the family, as when Dad went to Angola for two years and we had to stay at home for our safety, with my mother. Anyway, I grew up in London, Israel, Bangkok, Suffolk, Northern France, Johannesburg, Berne and Hamburg in that order.

One thing that was hampered by this way of life was the keeping of pets. We had some half-wild cats in the garden, during our sojourn in Suffolk while Dad was in Angola; and there was a period when my eldest brother and I kept white mice called Sid, Pugwash and Napoleon in the back shed; but we never had a dog or cat of our own. During our year in South Africa, we borrowed a dog called Tertia, a big soft golden bull mastiff; for years afterwards, I kept a curl of her yellow hair in my heart-shaped locket in her memory.

But the one pet who did stay with us, against all odds, was Birdie. Birdie's history was remarkable, and has always seemed to me to prove the triumphant nature of the life force; that a creature so small should cling to life so fiercely, and take such joy in it, was a marvel to us even then. He was a tiny African Finch. When my brother brought him home from his infant school, as a prize for being the quietest child during Rest Time, my mother was a bit appalled; we were told that they were a delicate breed, hard to keep in chilly northern climates, and that he

probably wouldn't live long. But he was a nice little thing, with a reddish head and a gay blue chest and brown wings, and we liked him. We bought a huge cage, the biggest we could find, and installed him in it in the kitchen. Rather to everyone's surprise, Birdie survived, and got livelier every day. We children, each in turn, learned to fill his feeding tube and replace the cuttlefish and sticks of millet in the cage. He never tried to get out, but perched on our fingers when we put them in to feed him. When the time came for the family to up stakes and move on (to South Africa, via Suffolk), Birdie came too, in the back of my mother's Citroen 2 CV. We were all adamant that he must come to South Africa, so my parents sheepishly enquired of the Union Castle line whether a bird might come as hand luggage? Yes indeed, said the mailship company. No trouble. He would be fed and looked after en route. And he was; the *Pendennis Castle* crew handed him over in Capetown a fortnight later, still chirruping.

The altitude of Johannesburg, right on the High Veldt 5,738ft above sea level, had been predicted as a certain killer for Birdie. It wasn't. He went on noshing into his millet and sharpening his little beak on his cuttlefish for the two years we lived there. When we came home, it was on a small cargo ship, the *Braemar Castle*, for a five-week journey up the East African coast and through the Suez Canal. The Captain agreed 'as long as I know nothing about it' that Birdie should hang in his cage in the chain locker on the Boat-Deck, and that we should feed him and look after him ourselves. I was by now thirteen years old, entering the troublesome world of the teenager; it was a restful thing at the end of a long shipboard day to go up on the highest deck and feed good old Birdie as the sun went down over Zanzibar, or Suez, or the Rock of Gibraltar. The view changed, he didn't.

And so he came home to Suffolk. There, on the kitchen windowsill, he chirped away his last year with us. He remained alone; at one point we had tried giving him a mate, hoping rather foolishly for eggs and chicks; but she died fairly soon, and Birdie showed no sign of caring much either way. He was obviously one of those cheerful confirmed bachelors who can't be bothered with the female sex. His wing-feathers went grey with age. My father got posted to Berne, and the elderly Birdie was boarded out back in Suffolk with a neighbour. I was busy, and concerned with the fate of my shedful of white mice and with my new life at a boarding-school in Kent; I'm afraid I don't remember feeling much when the news came of Birdie's death. But I haven't ever forgotten him. He spanned three countries and two hemispheres, and took me from the age of nine to the maturity of fourteen. In his small way, he mattered. I hope he enjoyed his life.

A LESSON IN SIN

RABBI LIONEL BLUE

AT SCHOOL I was called an unbelieving Jew, which was in fact true. I am now a very cautious believer, because I do not want to be religious cannon-fodder for anybody. This tendency has become stronger as I have become more professionally religious as well. Now, like many Jews, I am not cautious because I do not have the capacity to believe, but because like many Jews I am inclined to believe too much and too often, which, I suppose, is why we Jews are still here.

I shut my eyes and remember the kitchen table of my childhood. My grandmother believed, and she enjoyed it. She believed in God and wore a wig to please him. (As she tucked the housekeeping money under it, it was also useful, as in fact were most of her beliefs.) She believed in amulets for sickness and the evil eye, and, when I was a child, they did me good. She was also rash enough to believe in people, and so she had a life of belief, suffering and happiness. She was never burnt out by bitterness nor racked by envy, so her superstitions served her well. My grandfather on the other hand took a high view of God and a low view of his fellow Jews. He prayed regularly but refused to pay regularly, so he was unpopular with his synagogue. By contrast, he took things generously and gave them to beggars, including my mother's violin as she was working her way triumphantly through *Liebestraum.* It was odd that someone so cynical should have been a disciple of Prince Kropotkin, bravely asserting that the species helped each other to survive, which they might do in the Siberian forests he had left, but did not do so obviously in the East London dockland where he lived.

Then there were the assorted relations and friends, who gathered round my grandfather while he repaired shoes, and my grandmother when she made dumplings. I listened to them very carefully as a child, because, as they explained, they did not believe – they knew! Scientifically, like at school. They backed their knowledge with their lives, joining the noble army of secular saints and martyrs for materialism. Some of them were anarchist and returned to the East which they had left in childhood. They went to help the republic of goodness, which had got a bit confused, and we never heard of them again. I wonder what happened to their eager goodness, minced by the Stalinist machine. Well, they were told scientifically what would happen, by another crony who followed Trotsky. He was a little man who carried a great red banner. When the police came, everyone scuttled into houses and he was left out in the cold – the banner wouldn't go through the door – to take the consequences. When Trotsky was brained by an assassin, my childhood-friend gave

up his beliefs and took to business instead. He is, I think, successful but nostalgic. Other relations and friends migrated to Spain during the civil war, did what they thought was their duty, and when they did not come back, a great-aunt's hair turned white, and a woman in our street who had long memories of childhood pogroms went mad, gently but firmly. The thirties were so disastrous that it was a reasonable response.

I looked on a turbulent world, fascinated and frightened by the amount of goodness and absurdity in it. My father was a decent man, a strong and silent type, a gentleman with a rare and terrible temper for injustice. We were walking down Mile End, and my father saw a coloured man being thrown out of a pub. My father sailed in wearing his best suit, his arms flailing. There was uproar and the proprietor got knocked out. As he came to, he opened one eye and looked tenderly at my father. '*Heshl!*' he said in Yiddish, 'do you know why I was throwing the darkie out of the pub?' 'No,' said my father defensively. 'Well, he was making anti-semitic remarks.' It was unanswerable and he closed his eye. 'I told you so,' said my mother, mortified beyond endurance. It was like an Amen. I thought about it for a long time.

My father taught me swimming and he taught me sin. I still enjoy the first, but am truly grateful for the second lesson. To Christian readers the sin is not very terrible, to orthodox Jewish ones it still is. He was an inarticulate man, and through layers of embarrassment he asked me to come with him and not tell the family. We trudged in silence through dark and devious alleys and came to a shop where they sold jellied eels, strictly forbidden in Jewish Law. There were only men there, and it was my father's only escape from the meshes of matriarchy and tradition which governed our lives. He had suffered the dole and the loss of his dignity. He also knew that as I became more educated I would grow away from him. Before I had completely gone beyond recall, he took me to his private place, the only one he had. He was respected there, he recovered his manhood, and he talked. The truth which is not always welcome in liturgy could shine out among jellied eels. Should I give him away? I had a battle between priggishness and common sense. Thank God common sense won, and it is the only way I like to remember him now.

From this warm chaos I learnt a number of things. I learnt that reality was real and very solid. You could dream what you liked, but it would not change. I knew that no prayers would get people off the trains to concentration camps, and wishing would never make it so, despite religion or popular songs; it was the same syrup whether it came in full canonicals or from a juke box. When Mosley marched through the East End I prayed very hard. He didn't get through, but I gave the credit to my father who landed in hospital, my grandfather who landed in the arms of the police, and my grandmother's old cronies who carried buckets of water to throw from first-floor windows in Aldgate. My frightened piety had more to do with pixies and garden gnomes, and even as a child I never took it seriously. This suspicion of piety has remained with me.

from A Backdoor to Heaven

YOUNG TALES FROM THE RAJ

GORDON HONEYCOMBE

IWAS BORN IN India, in the last years of the British Raj, three years before the start of the Second World War. My father had gone out to India in 1925 to work for an American oil company, Standard-Vac. He moved from Bombay to Karachi, eventually becoming the Sales Manager there, and it was there in a far and very foreign country, that my parents married, in December 1927. They were both 29. My mother, as far as I know, had never been out of Scotland before, and she hadn't seen my father for two years. The long voyage out was only a prelude to considerable changes in her life, far from the cheerful and often chilly confines of a Scottish village. My sister was born in Karachi (now of course in Pakistan) in 1930 and I in September 1936.

We lived on the edge of Karachi, in Bath Island Road, in a two-storey mansion divided into four flats and rented from a Parsee family. Our flat was on the first floor. There was a wide, enclosed verandah at the front, overlooking a fairly formal, dusty garden. At the rear, a spiral iron staircase led down from the kitchen to a yard and the servants' quarters, which were mixed up with the garages and where we did not venture. We had three permanent servants (and there were only four of us). We had a *bearer* (butler), a *hamal* (houseboy), and a cook. All three wore loose white garments, and the first two had turbaned headgear and thick moustaches. The cook, who was clean-shaven and younger than the other two, wore an early version of a T-shirt and shorts. He was much darker-skinned and must have come from southern India. In his small hot kitchen, where there was a clay oven, I was allowed to make *chapathis*. I remember nothing about the food we ate, whether British or Indian, except that at Sunday lunch we had tasty chicken pilaus, with nuts, raisins and a spicy but watery tomato sauce. The servants were kind to the master's only son, the *chota-sahib* (small master), caring and respectful. I remember how baffled I was on the day we left Karachi, when the *hamal*, whom I had only viewed as a servant, seized my hand and wept.

With the occupants of the other three flats (all British apart from the Parsee owners) we shared the *mali* (gardener) and the *dhobi* (washerman). I also had an *ayah* (nanny) up to the age of six. The one I remember was plump and even darker-skinned than the cook. She washed and dressed me and went with me on visits, consorting nearby with other *ayahs*, while I played with other children, in their

homes, outside, or at fancy-dress parties, or pestered my mother as she joked with friends at the Gymkhana. This was a well-run social club, where there were swings, lawns, tennis courts, lounges, dining rooms, a billiards room, a library and a bar. It was a popular meeting place for British families at the weekend, and also for the adults in the evening after work. I was never taken there then. On Sunday mornings an Indian pipe-band in full dress tartan paraded up and down on the grass before the terrace. There were other clubs: the Country Club, the Sind Club and the Boat Club – where I learned apprehensively to swim in the dark, water-snake and crab-infested waters of the creek by the clubhouse, in whose wicker-chaired, airy rooms I would avidly consume, until rebuked, peanuts and small brown sausages dipped in tomato sauce.

At other weekends families would pile into motor cars and drive north out of Karachi (a small town made bigger by business headquarters, busy docks, government and military establishments), to a long sandy stretch of the coast where beach huts dotted the low dunes above the shore. Here we would spend a night or two, roughing it without any servants, picnicking during the war years on tins of corned beef, beetroot and peaches, all favourites of mine. Apart from an afternoon siesta we were out of doors most of the time, on the beach and in the sea, with my head protected from the sun by an outsize topee, and my skinny frame garbed in a one-piece swim-suit. Mounds of stranded jellyfish could be found on the shore and strange dead fish, sometimes turtles and their eggs. Once I nearly drowned when paddling too far out in the warm frothy ocean, overwhelmed by a breaker and dragged away in the undertow. I disappeared. All that the adults suddenly saw was my topee floating on the sea. Found and rescued, choking and gasping, I was borne ashore, screaming blue murder when I could.

In 1939, when war was declared, I was three. It hardly impinged on my childhood, apart from the plethora of tinned, mostly American foods, and the collections we children were urged to make for the War Effort (whatever that was) of bottle-tops and tins and silver paper. Men in uniform were common enough; some visited our flat; some were to be seen at clubs and beaches. But I never associated them with events elsewhere. Europe meant nothing to me. Burma meant something – it was somewhere near India, though still a million miles from our blue horizons. A people called the Japs were seemingly to be feared. But the grown-ups' talk was generally meaningless, in this and in virtually everything. I was too young to listen to the wireless, although I responded to the popular songs and military music I occasionally heard. I never read newspapers, just comics, like *Superman* and *Captain Marvel*; and of course there was no television. There were films; and in the cinema I sat entranced beside my mother, agog in the dark on sunny afternoons at the mind-boggling, emotional mysteries of such wartime entertainments as *Eagle Squadron, Wake Island, Mrs Miniver, Lost Horizon* and *Gone With the Wind.* 'You can go, but I'm staying,' I told my mother, when she thought I had had enough at the interval.

Gordon Honeycombe, his mother and pith helmet going for a ride in Karachi

There was also the special, sad magic of Disney films, like *Snow White* and *Bambi*, and *The Wizard of Oz*; and there was Charlie Chaplin in *The Gold Rush* and *The Cure*. My father had a whirring ciné-projector at home, and these Chaplin films and others, shown to children squatting on the carpet, usually at parties, with black and white cartoons, always ensured hilarity. Laurel and Hardy were never as good.

The only wartime excitement I recall was when a section of the Indian Navy mutinied, and a cruiser in Karachi harbour fired blank shells over the town – at least, I was told they were blanks.

Except for the steamy monsoon rains and the dust-storms, the sun always shone. Shirt, shorts and sandals were worn throughout the year. But I was never aware of it being hot (being cold was quite unknown), although I sometimes got overheated, uncomfortable and tired. There seemed to be no night, just day, and I was outside most of the time. My mother was apparently little concerned about me being harmed by any Indian. She made a fuss about sunstroke, about drinking tap-water, and rabid dogs. I had a great deal of freedom, being allowed, so it seems now, to roam at will around the neighbourhood from about the time I went to school.

It was a kind of kindergarten, run by two Misses Carter, sisters, in a room in their house near the railway line. Lessons lasted for only a couple of hours each morning, and in between drawing, modelling with plasticine and playing games, I

learned to read, write, add up and do the multiplication table. My imagination had already been caught by the pictures in the Beatrix Potter books (Pigling Bland was my particular hero). Now I could read the stories. I devoured them all, as well as *Babar the Elephant* and the picture books of Alison Uttley, before progressing to A.A. Milne, Lewis Carroll, and all the Biggles, Just William and Swallows and Amazons books I could find. Before I left India in April 1946, I had begun to write: short poems first of all, and Chapter One of a story called *Mole*.

By then I was 9½, and grown up, mainly in inches. I didn't know what I was leaving, nor what lay ahead in a cold and distant northern country. Still less did I realise that within a year this most marvellous and most British part of the Empire would be partitioned, with the consequent wholesale movement and slaughter of millions. Our *hamal* would have been aware of the imminent end of the old order, and that he would never see the *chota-sahib* again. I remained blissfully unaware that I was leaving not only my childhood in the heat and dust of Bath Island Road.

The previous summer we had holidayed in the lower Himalayas, at Naini Tal, and while returning with my mother and a small friend from an afternoon showing of an Errol Flynn film, *They Died With Their Boots On*, I became mixed up in a demonstration. My mother drew down the blinds of the rickshaw, shutting out the rioting crowds, though not the noise. It all meant less to me than the film, which had been much more alarming and real. I never thought of danger. For we were British after all: invulnerable, as we had always been, and uninvolved.

THE PYJAMA GAME

TONY HART

BOTH MY BROTHER and I were at the same school in Dorset, but at different times. We had enjoyed our days there particularly as the school was, and is, noted for its encouragement of art and drama. I remember with pleasure the somewhat decrepit art studio reeking of linseed oil and turpentine, and spent a lot of time there. The art master was also the school chaplain. A notable artist who would get the best out of those boys who were interested and wanted to work. My housemaster, as well as running the House and teaching, was a keen typographer who ran a most effective printshop for the school. This was attached to the art studio and probably accounted for my interest in graphic art and, ultimately, my work in this area of the world of art.

My brother, following on three years later, showed little interest in the art studio but soon became one of a worthy company whose main interest was with the school theatre. The theatre was, if possible, even more decrepit than the art studio. It too was a part of that extraordinary complex. The seating in the auditorium had come from a disused cinema; not one seat was in anything like a good state of repair and the stage and all that went with it left a great deal to be desired. For all that, some excellent productions were staged. I remember playing Cecily in *The Importance of Being Earnest*. The part of Gwendoline being played by, the now, Norroy and Ulster King of Arms! My brother, in his day, had played Ophelia. But Michael's interest in the theatre went further than acting. He worked on the lighting board, stage carpentry and even helped organise a touring company, and during those wartime days brought a bit more drama to the outlying villages – mostly on foot. In due course he became an actor and is now a television producer.

After the war, I returned from the Far East and revisited my old school. It was late afternoon, in summer. The great chestnut tree (with my initials on a topmost branch) cast its shadow over the lawn in front of my old House. There, chatting together in the last of the day's sun, were my housemaster and the school chaplain. They both looked exactly the same. I walked towards them across the grass. 'Ah,' said my housemaster. 'Hart, N.A.' It was a statement not a question. I was delighted that he recognised me after those years. The chaplain remembered too. 'How,' he asked, 'is your brother, Hart, M.C.?' 'Fine,' I told him. 'He's in *The Pyjama Game*.' There was a pause while this was considered. 'Ah,' said my housemaster again. 'Ah, well. I suppose somebody has to make them.'

What an extraordinary, close, inward-looking little world they live in, I thought. But that was nearly forty years ago. Now I'm much more inclined to believe that they knew exactly what their old boys had done and were doing. My old art master is no longer with us, though his paintings are. But my housemaster's dry wit was still in evidence at the last O.C's reunion!

COUNTRY-BOYS' GAMES

LAURIE LEE

AS GLOUCESTERSHIRE BOYS, the games and rituals we played seemed to run through the natural order of the seasons.

Most games we played for our amusement only; rituals were traditional and sometimes earned us some pocket money.

At the start of the year, we had 'first footing' – the habit of crossing a neighbour's threshold early in the morning and wishing them 'Good Luck and a Happy New Year!'

It was always best if you were the first to call; even better if you had black hair. A 'dark stranger', for some reason, was considered to be a symbol of good fortune; those of us with fair hair carried a lump of coal.

With the New Year past came the time of inexhaustible pleasures with the landscape wrapped up in snow and ice. The generosity of snow always seemed unbounded – you could eat it, drink it, throw it about, make caves or tunnels in it, cut it into slabs, build steps or walls or houses.

Country snow seemed always clean and white as paper, so that you could read things in it, track birds, badgers or even foxes, as well as the big hob-nailed boots of your friends.

As long as the hard winter lasted, our games were many and traditional – playing the xylophone on icicles hanging from the roofs, or licking the same like lollipops; and best of all, if the ice was strong enough, working up a slide across the village pond which, when perfectly polished, was a magic carpet that bore one in an effortless dream through the landscape.

Next, while the frosts still held and the roads were not yet turned to mud, came the time for whipping tops up and down the village – wooden rainbow tops, painted in bright reds and greens, so that when they spun, the colours melted together in a dazzle of changing hues.

The whips were simple lengths of string or long strips of leather stolen from one's sister's tall lace-up boots. The top was set in the dust, its point screwed in the ground, then whipped sharply so that it flew high through the air. If whipped properly it would settle and spin like a humming bird rocking and quivering gently.

To keep it alive one ran and whipped it again, and then it would rise singing, and spin even faster, and might strike sparks from the stony road when it landed. On the other hand, it could also sky through a window, or get caught in the whiplash and snap back and give you a bonk on the head.

Later, before the general thaw began, came the time for the bowling of hoops;

and these made sparks too when driven along the road, because our hoops were made of iron. I am talking of the days when our roads weren't tarred but were surfaced with little stones and flints. Our iron hoops could strike up brilliant streams of sparks if sent at the proper angles across the stones. They could also be instruments of danger if they got out of control, and could cut open the knee to the bone. But we boys thought no less of them for that, and were proud of their speed and power. The girls, on the other hand, were only allowed light hoops of cane, which we boys, of course, thought sissy . . .

Many of our games were played in the middle of the roads, which, since there was no traffic in those days – except for an occasional horse and cart, or an old man with a wheelbarrow – were considered a perfectly safe place to be.

Here, squatting on our knees in a circle, we played 'knuckle-bones' or 'five-stones', a game older than Shakespeare, a game of manual dexterity, almost a feat of juggling, fiercely competitive and with many extended variations.

Traditional 'knuckle-bones' was played with the knuckles of pigs' feet, but as we, for the most part, were too poor to eat meat, we played with little stones instead.

The game consisted of tossing the stones in the air, catching them on the back of the hand, manipulating some on the ground while still keeping at least one in the air, grabbing, scraping and catching till the game was over.

The mysteries of 'five-stones' and 'knuckle-bones' are too complex to explain fully, unless you happened to be born into them. They required a nimbleness, a sleight-of-hand sufficient to dazzle the eye; and the girls – it must be admitted – were better at it than we were. (But so they were at hopscotch – a game older than the Pyramids – but then that was considered to be a 'girls' game' anyway.

Summer games were perhaps slower but no less various than others – snail-racing, an indolent pastime as one can imagine; 'french-cricket', played along pathways using one's legs as stumps; warfare with grass seeds catapulted from the bent looped stem; fishing for tiddlers; and 'fox-and-hounds' in the moonlight.

Then, with autumn, came 'conkers' – a classic battle of determination and nerve – with the shiny brown chestnuts hanging on strings and then brutally bashed against each other in turn. Four things could happen in this encounter. Either the striker missed his opponent altogether, or the strings got entangled and caused an awkward pause, or both conkers colliding smashed each other to pieces, or one or other of them emerged victorious.

The veteran survivor of many battles took on the value of the conkers he'd vanquished, so that you'd get a 'two-er', a 'twelver', even a 'fortyer', according to your various successes. I saw a 'fiftyer' once, a sharp-edged little nut looking grey and hard as a stone. I thought it to be deathless or an invincible destroyer – but some said it had been baked in an oven . . .

In autumn, too, was the time when we made bows and arrows – perhaps a tribute to the hunting season. Our bows were made of light springy willow, and our

arrows cut from a hazel bush, straight peeled and sharpened at the end. If properly strung and used with average skill it was astonishing how powerful these bows and arrows could be, light and far-ranging as those of Persian cavalry or the mounted warriors of the Tartars. At the day's end, I remember, we'd often stand in the blue gloom of the valley and shoot an arrow vertically into the sky, and watch it climb, climb, till it caught the light of the setting sun, and hang there for a moment, gold and illuminated, before turning to plunge back into the evening's shadow.

Then Winter and Christmas would be on us again, with snow-balling and carol-singing; but I always think that that slender arrow, hanging in the sun's last glow, was the magic symbol of the Fall of the year.

MESSING ABOUT IN CARS

BARRY TOOK

I WAS RUN OVER when I was five years old. Not fatally, of course, but knocked down I was and disappeared, to my mother's horror, under a car being driven at a modest speed up our suburban street. My survival is due to the fact that the road, or rather Avenue to give it its due, on a new estate in North London, had not yet been tarmacadamised and was a riot of potholes. It was into one of these holes in the road that I was knocked and came out comparatively unscathed.

The motorist drove my mother and me to the doctor's where I was pronounced grazed, bruised and shaken but otherwise intact, and on the way back from the surgery it is reported that I sang a tune popular at the time, 'Ain't It Grand To Be Blooming Well Dead'!

When I was very young cars had an almost hypnotic attraction for me. At the age of three I climbed into the driver's seat of a van parked on the steep hill on which we lived and released the handbrake. The van unsurprisingly ran briskly backwards down the hill across a mercifully quiet main road and demolished some railings that surrounded the local school.

Eighteen months or so later I did exactly the same thing with another vehicle (a laundry van this time – the first one had been delivering groceries) and that careered into a neighbour's wall. After those early encounters with motor transport it's hardly

surprising that I was never entirely happy in motor cars and, in fact, didn't learn to drive until I was nearly thirty.

In those days, the early thirties, cars were becoming popular and the Sunday drive and the day at the seaside were commonplace. My father's first car was a tiny saloon that was forever breaking down so that when we set off, however hopefully, we never actually expected to arrive and when we did make it to our destination, Whipsnade Zoo for instance, or the village of Chipperfield, or Southend on Sea, the whole family shared my father's sense of achievement at actually having made it. Later my father got a more reliable model and a lot of the adventure went out of our excursions, until with the coming of war in 1939, and petrol rationing, the car went under wraps for the duration. In spite of my early adventures with lorries, memories of my early youth are mainly of horse-drawn vehicles. The coalman, the milkman, the baker all had horse-drawn vans and I remember too a travelling grocery (could it have been Carwardines?) which would grind its way up and down the hilly roads of New Southgate dispensing whatever grocers dispensed in those days.

Many of the products have vanished, or at least I haven't seen Eiffel Tower pudding or Icilma face cream, or Betox savoury spread, or De Reske Minor cigarettes ('the ten minute smoke for intelligent folk') since the forties. Mind you, I rarely go shopping and haven't smoked for years so I may just be out of touch.

A great treat for us children was a ride on the milkman's cart and it was a red letter day when the milkman actually let you hold the reins as the horse ambled its accustomed route, stopping and starting where it chose. But best of all was a ride on the coal cart – slow, dirty but enchanting, and even today I can remember the *smell* of the coal and the sacks and being ticked off more than once for arriving home dirty and late having wheedled a lift from the coalman.

I look back at these innocent pleasures with nostalgia tinged with wonder. It seems so dull in comparison with what children enjoy today but it didn't seem so then, and looking back must have been anything but dull for my poor parents at the height of my van-pranging days.

FIRST LOVES

MONICA DICKENS

I HAVE BEEN IN love with somebody ever since I can remember; usually several people at once, if you count hero worship.

My first love was my father. I can hear now the crash of the London front door as he came exuberantly home from the Law Courts, and his voice sailing up the stairs, 'Where's my baby?'

I slid down to him on my bottom, which was the quickest way to go at that age, but it wasn't long, alas, before I learned my power as the beloved, and would stand halfway down the stairs and shout, 'No come see My Baby. Go down write papers,' to make him beg me.

I was in love with my brother, ten years older than me and stunning in his naval cadet's uniform, who taught me jokes: 'One rode a horse and the other rhododendron', the wittiest thing I had ever heard. Then I was in love with my handsome cousin and countless other people I had never met. When I could read and write, I kept a list of them under my pillow, and would tell them over to myself, like prayers, before I went to sleep.

The Prince of Wales. A haggard young officer in the play, *Journey's End*, with a blood-stained bandage round his head and one arm in a sling. St George of the Raphael picture, spearing the dragon from his white horse, who looks back at him with the round, limpid eyes of an adoring woman. Gerald du Maurier as the romantic father in *Dear Brutus*, with me as the dream daughter: 'Daddy, I don't want to be a might-have-been!' A local policeman. A musical comedy hero who ended his song of frustrated love by staggering to the footlights and crying, 'Bernice!' to me where I sat in the third row of the stalls on my birthday treat. Faces seen in newspapers, on posters, dashing young men in silks at steeplechases. They all went on my list.

Monica (left) great-granddaughter of Charles Dickens

From the age of ten when I got my first pony, the loves were overshadowed by the overwhelming passion for horses, which has stayed with me all my life.

Chips, Jenny, Gemma, Little David, Meg, Over Again, Bow Window, Jackie, Bobby, Ben, Guy, John, David Copperfield, Robin . . . I've loved about fifty

horses and ponies, and it is their names I tell over to myself now sometimes when I can't sleep.

After I went to St Paul's, weekends and holidays were still horses, but the week was Fiona McLeod, Captain of Netball, and Comfort Turner, Captain of Gym, and other glamorous heroines in gym tunics, who may or may not have known that the small blushing girl who kept turning up in corridors and round corners would have fainted dead away if they had said, 'Hello'. Perhaps that was why they didn't.

The pure loves of childhood can be as sweet and painful as the complicated turmoil of grown-up emotions and desires for which they are the prologue. The turning point was a farmyard in Oxfordshire when a boy with whom I had been childishly jumping off a haystack grabbed me in the loose hay and kissed me violently.

The world stood still. The sky reeled above my open, astonished eyes. No loves were ever quite the same again.

PUTTING ON THE GLOVES

FRANK KEATING

HAD I BEEN aware of the crucially outstanding work the NSPCC had been doing since 1884, I would certainly have rung them from a Berkshire call-box one afternoon in the winter of 1950. I was a pale and spindly urchin just into my teens. My knees still turn to old rope at the memory. But let me begin at the beginning . . .

Perhaps because I am both a weed and a drip, I have always been wretchedly beguiled by the *theory* and heroism of prizefighting. Hard as I try, I cannot resist the drama of the so-called Noble Art and, as a sportswriter now, you will always find me, full of anticipation, at the ringside before any big fight. Perhaps, unconsciously, I got my first fix, my baptismal buzz, when I was only a few days old – for Tommy Farr fought Joe Louis in the week that I was born, in the Autumn of 1937, when half of Britain stayed up to listen on new-fangled little walnut wireless sets to the first-ever live relay of a sporting event from America. Something might have rubbed off . . . certainly by the end of the war I was listening on my crystal set at nights to such broadcast epics as Woodcock v Baksi, Woodcock v Savold, Mills v Lesnevitch,

Turpin v Robinson . . . with Macpherson or Glendenning spitting out the descriptions faster than the poor boxers were teeth.

When I was about ten, Dad and Uncle John took me to see the fights one night at Gloucester Baths. Perhaps they thought it would cure me. The heat, the din, the cigar smoke, the *blood* . . . It did. Temporarily. I fainted, and was carried out flat as a board like the original horizontal British heavyweight, Phil Scott, who they used to call Faintin' Phil, the Dying Swan of Soho.

At twelve, I went to Douai, a Benedictine monastery school high in the blissful Berkshire hills above Newbury. I pinned my poster of Ezzard Charles to the inside door of my dormitory bedside cupboard (all the others had Betty Grable or Piper Laurie), and I joined the Boxing Club, run by a ferocious drill-master called Sgt Hartigan, and a kindly, myopic priest called Father Augustine. Every Tuesday and Thursday evening I sparred in the gym with another boxing nut called Pite; we'd dance around each other, taking it in turns to commentate like Glendenning, and to snort when we threw a left, to grunt when we swung a right, and occasionally we went down on one knee for the count of nine. But, all the while, of course, *we never once landed a real blow*. It was just boyhood bravado and make-believe.

But it sure impressed the gangly Benedictine myopic, Fr Augustine. He put me in the team for the school's first match against Bradfield, the snooty neighbouring boarding-school. I still did not suspect. I had the regulation butterflies-in-my-tummy when the school bus set off, but consoled myself that Randy had had them too when he left the dressing-room to beat Albert Finch the week before. I had read that in the *Sunday Dispatch*.

We changed into our white strip, with the purple sash. All my senior-school heroes wished me luck, for as the 'Paperweight' I was first on. The rest of the team sat in the front row waiting their turn. It was necessary Douai got away to a good start, said Fr Augustine as he gloved me up. Three one-minute rounds. The whistle went – and suddenly this *giant* in the blue sash, whom I had just tremulously shaken hands with, hit me on the nose harder than I've ever been hit before. Or since, come to think of it. My eyes watered and my nose started hosing blood. Then he hit me in the solar plexus. I think I let out a piercing scream. The whistle went early by about 47 seconds. I was crumpled and squatting against my corner ringpost with my arms wrapped around my head. I had not, in fact, taken even half a step forward.

Fr Augustine went to retrieve his towel from the centre of the ring, then brought it back, roughly to mop up my blood, cold sweat, and tears. 'You are nothing less,' he sneered, 'than a total disgrace to the school!'

It was the end of my career in the ring. Mind you, I'm still hot stuff outside it.

STAR SECRET

TWIGGY

ONE OF MY earliest recollections is going to the television studios with my mum when I was about six. A painting of mine, 'The Queen Going For A Walk', had been chosen for a children's exhibition in the National Gallery, and as a prize I had been invited to watch a production of the Rolf Harris Show, and also to meet some of the artists appearing. Rolf Harris was exceptionally nice and he has remained a firm favourite of mine, and it's strange now that my own daughter, Carly, who is nearly eight, is a big fan of his.

I also met there a lovely lady, Alma Cogan, who sadly is no longer alive, but then was a very big star and everyone seemed to be a fan of hers. It was then that I got one of my biggest thrills, which I still remember vividly even now. Alma Cogan took me aside and whispered that she was going to tell me a secret that no one else would know, and could I keep it very much to myself. I could only nod, as I was too shy to speak, and she told me that she was going to wear in her next television show a special gold dress, and that I was the only person in the world who would know beforehand.

Winning third prize in a baby show

I couldn't believe my ears that she had given me such a tremendous secret, and with some difficulty I managed to keep it until the time for her show came around. When she appeared, wearing the gold dress, I felt that she was singing and speaking just to me alone, and she created a very magical moment which time has not eroded.

Alma is still very sadly missed, but at least she has left some wonderful memories – particularly to someone who can still remember being six whenever she thinks of that beautiful, glamorous, gold dress.

EARLIEST MEMORIES

DONALD TRELFORD

THE CLEVEREST MAN I ever knew used to claim, in all seriousness, that his earliest memory – a vivid one, he used to insist – was of being held up and spanked the moment after birth. He stuck to this story against all kinds of derision and disbelief for as long as he lived. I cannot claim to go back in memory as far as that myself, but I do have a first mental snapshot that is equally vivid. I can date it precisely: 15 November, 1940, just six days after my third birthday.

I can place it precisely too. It was on the road that runs down the side of Coventry Council House towards St Mary's Hall and the Cathedral, just off Earl Street. It was the morning after the Coventry Blitz, when German bombers took the heart out of the city and destroyed the old Cathedral as they fire-bombed the armament factories.

My grandfather drove me round the city the morning after the raid in the old brown Austin Seven – OG 7041, I can still recall – in which he used to do his rounds making door-to-door deliveries of 'Trelford's Teas'. I think I remember the experience so strongly because he kept telling me to 'look at this, boy; never forget what you're seeing now', he would say to the three-year-old toddler in the back.

Not that I would have needed much encouragement to remember, with high buildings still burning around me, water and sand all over the streets, and blanketed bundles, which I later learned to be corpses, set out carefully on top of the rubble to await collection. The worst scenes were long since over, but some of the buildings were being allowed to burn themselves out while the firemen attended to more urgent business.

My father was away in the Army at the time, waiting for embarkation orders to the Middle East. When he heard the heavily censored news of the Coventry raid, he went absent without leave and travelled from Aldershot by night through the black-out to see if his family were alive and his house still standing. He found the house deserted and the family gone, which must have been an awful shock until he learnt from neighbours that I had been evacuated to the country with my mother, who was about to give birth to my sister. He wasn't to see the new baby until he returned from overseas several years later.

My other recollection of childhood is a less sombre one. The story has been recounted since by my mother with great hilarity, but that can hardly have been her reaction at the time.

A friend and I were always daring each other to do the most dangerous things –

in fact, I can hardly think back on those escapades even now without a shudder of fright. For example, we would have an air rifle and take turns to fire it at the other – the 'target' being stationed behind a fence at the bottom of the garden with one eye or a flash of forehead showing through a knot-hole in the wood. The gunman would then aim several rounds at the knot-hole.

Another 'game' was for one of us to swing on a gate while the other aimed darts at the moving leg – and since we were in short trousers, there was nothing at all to protect us. Both of us had to pick out a dart on occasions – naturally without a murmur.

The one my mother remembers best (perhaps because she didn't know about the others) took place one hot summer afternoon when we were feeling bored. We stood on the sill of my first-floor bedroom window and dared each other to leap over the washing line, which hung over a concrete yard, and onto the small patch of lawn beyond. As she came up the stairs, my mother could hear us debating the challenge. It suddenly dawned on her what we were planning to do and she rushed into the bedroom to stop us. Too late – all that met her horrified maternal eyes was the sight of the curtains flapping gently in the light breeze from the open window. She dashed to look out, fearing the worst – only to see two tiny boys rolling around laughing on the grass. We'd made it – though, as I remember, she wasn't too impressed about that. My young partner, incidentally, is now a JP.

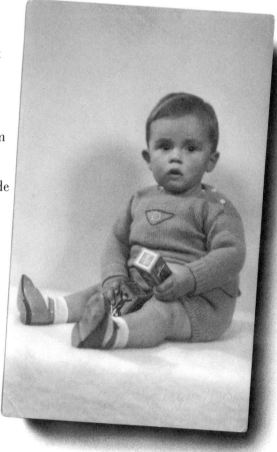

The editor of the Observer, aged 2

MIDNIGHT FEAST

GLENYS KINNOCK

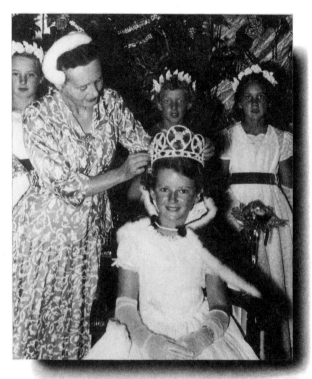

Carnival Queen, aged 12

WHEN I WAS a child, all the books I read seemed to be about heroic children whose whole lives were spent having adventures and solving mysteries.

One half-term holiday when I was about nine a group of us met regularly in a garden shed, called ourselves the Secret Six and waited for something to happen.

Of course a small town in North Wales does not offer many opportunities for the kind of adventure handed out to Enid Blyton's heroes. We decided to manufacture some of our own – a midnight feast.

We 'acquired' packets of biscuits and soft drinks from our pantries at home and stored them carefully in our Garden Shed HQ.

My problem was how to get out in the middle of the night and how to get back after the nocturnal feasting. I managed to sneak my mother's key out of her purse and then I innocently went up to bed at about 8.30pm. Of course I didn't bother to undress but lay in there listening for my father to go out to work. My mother always went to bed early when he was on night shift at the signal box. To my horror I heard the sound of the electric sewing machine and realised that that night of all nights she was planning to stay downstairs.

There was no alternative but to take the risk and leave in order to make the rendezvous time. I put my pillows lengthways in my bed, held my breath and crept downstairs – timing each creak with the sound of the machine.

I ran through the dark, deserted streets, reached my friend's house, climbed over the garden wall and found them all whispering nervously in the candle-lit shed.

We were all too frightened to enjoy the feast and wondered why we were not as brave as the children in the stories.

I braced myself to begin the five-minute run home. I found the house in darkness, turned the key in the lock and with my heart pounding reached the safety of my bedroom.

It was years later before I retold the story to my family – when it was too late for punishment!

DEMON DRINK

SIR FRED HOYLE

A CHILD SOON LEARNS it has a special relationship with its mother, and with its father a little while later, but it is not until the age of about three that the child perceives a similar relationship for others. Then it does so mostly for children whom it meets and plays with, who can also be seen to have mothers and fathers. Grandparents are quite a problem to fit into place, especially as there may be two sets of them. The concept that one's own parents also have parents is an awkward one. In my own case this critical aspect of life was made still more awkward by the fact that, while both my grandmothers lived close by in Gilstead, neither of my grandfathers was still alive, so there were no obvious pairings to be spotted. George Hoyle, my paternal grandfather, came from Rochdale in Lancashire. Like so many menfolk in the district he earned his living in the textile business, but his real interests, according to older relatives who knew him, were in mathematics and chess.

I was never able in my youth to sort out the larger family relationships which, from listening to my parents, I realised I possessed. My paternal grandparents had both been married before, so as well as my own direct line there were children from two sets of former marriages. I had great grandparents with a family of thirteen, some lines of which had proliferated further. The details seemed too amazing to be true. I was somehow related to the Hammond family of Bradford, which owned Hammond's Brewery and counted itself among the plutocracy of the district. I do not recall seeing a Hammond, although every day in my teens I passed billboards on my way to school which bore big posters that read 'Hammond Ales', displaying a hefty fellow drinking from a large tankard, posters which were plastered throughout the Bradford area. I would pause in front of one of them to search my empty jacket in the hope that a

coin might have slipped through a hole into the inner lining, and would think to myself how fine it must be to own a brewery. The Hammonds were elusive people. I learned in later life that they had sent their carriage to my great-grandfather's funeral, but didn't attend themselves, despite the relationship and despite his being regarded as one of the outstanding Yorkshire poets of his day.

Better known to me was my Uncle Harry, actually my Great Uncle Harry, who visited my parents from time to time. I always liked Great Uncle Harry, even though he dressed in rags. The rags seemed less important to me than his invariably complimentary remark: 'Now *there's* a grand lad.' On one of his visits my mother was having trouble in shutting a warped door. Knowing Uncle Harry was supposed to have received training as a joiner my mother permitted him to fix it, which he rapidly did by slicing away at the door with an axe, much to my father's grief when he came home in the evening. Like me, Uncle Harry didn't have two penny pieces to rub together, because if he was ever so fortunate he immediately made his way at the double to the nearest pub. A time came when the family decided Uncle Harry's rags were not helpful to its own social standing. So they fitted him out with a resplendent new suit, only for the suit to disappear within the week, doubtless into the hands of a pawnbroker. To the family's frenzied demand to know what had happened to the suit, Uncle Harry declared that it had blown away in a strong wind on Saltaire Bridge, and from this view of what had transpired he could not be budged; the seeds of imaginative greatness must have lain tragically dormant in my Great Uncle Harry.

Then there was Black Uncle Jack, actually my Great Uncle Jack, who my father always insisted was much the strongest man in the district. I never saw Uncle Jack, but stories of his prowess lit up my young life as the nightime tipping of molten iron from a furnace lights up the clouds overhead. After a day's work, Black Uncle Jack would become blind drunk. He was not welcome in the local pubs because in such situations he would flay alive anybody who should contradict him in the smallest degree. The nearest character I have come on in world literature to my Great Uncle Jack was Brandy Bottle Bates in the stories of Damon Runyon. There was, I believe, general relief in the district when one dark night, following just such a combative evening, my Great Uncle Jack fell on his way home into the local canal, and became 'drowned-dead', as Charles Dickens' Mr Peggotty would have said. This was the Leeds-to-Liverpool canal, the 'cut' as it was known in the local vernacular.

There is no way a person could judge today from visiting a modern pub how beer drinking used to be in the good old days. There was a middle-aged man in my village, not a relative this time, of whom most drinkers stood in some awe. He heard one evening of a pub some four miles away which was opening that very evening under new management and in the interests of goodwill was dispensing free beer. With a thunderous cry of, 'Why didn't anybody tell'm?' he raced out of the village and downhill pell-mell into the town of Bingley, where he set off, still in full cry, in the direction of Crossflatts. He was said to have reached the pub at half past nine.

Half an hour later, at the statutory closing time of ten o'clock, he rolled out of the pub into the street, ten pints of beer to the good – or to the bad, as the temperance folk saw it.

Life was so closed in by what we would regard today as severe poverty and by a lack of communications – closed in except for the local cinema for which one paid 1*d* or 0.4p to gain entrance into what was popularly known as the 'bug hole' – that a large majority of the menfolk spent their evenings in the pubs. Beer in those days was priced at only a penny or two to the pint; at such low cost, drinking was necessarily excessive, and the tendency was for the male population to be formed into two disparate groups – either you drank to excess or you didn't drink at all. I do not recall a commercially produced alcoholic beverage ever being brought into our house. This wasn't because my parents were doctrinaire about alcohol the way some people were, but because they saw it as an all or nothing situation.

A Mr Bartle came to live in our village. He was an extreme temperance advocate. Between the ages of eight and twelve I saw quite a bit of Mr Bartle, a man with a cherry-red nose, because his house was close by, and partly because in co-operation with the local church he made temperance propaganda among us young fry. The organisation in question was called the Band of Hope, a title more frank in its honesty than most. The main consideration was that if we joined the Band of Hope we obtained the use of a large warm church hut in winter on a particular night of the week, Tuesday I think. There were clear bribes from time to time of buns and cakes, consumed with much speed and relish. Also from time to time there were harangues from visiting personages, which even in my tender years I couldn't help viewing with a certain morbid fascination. A singer in a stiff collar stands out sharply in my memory, a singer who rendered the toreador's song from *Carmen* accompanied by piano and trumpet, an occasion not to be missed. More routinely, we would be shown lantern slides of drops of water and alcohol, the water teeming with ugly-looking creatures, the alcohol devoid of such things. 'There,' the lecturer would say, 'nothing can live in alcohol,' whereon Mr Bartle would intone in a sombre voice, 'Never let a drop of it pass your lips.' Meanwhile some of us would have realised there were other very different interpretations of what we had just seen.

From *The Small World of Fred Hoyle*

SHELL SHOCK

ALAN COREN

*I*HAD A GOOD war, all in all.

Picked up a bit of shrapnel, of course, but who didn't? There was a lot of it flying about, then. You didn't make a fuss.

'*What's that, Coren?*'

'Nothing, sir. Bit of shrapnel.'

'*Shrapnel, eh? Better take a look.*'

'It's only – ow!'

'*What do I do to boys who pick up dangerous things?*'

'You clout them with Old Tom, sir.'

'*I clout them with Old Tom, correct.*'

It still smarts in wet weather.

What kind of madman calls his stick Old Tom? Nobody in 2a knew for certain why our dear form-master had not been called up, but the strong suspicion was that he was being held in reserve in case Hitler pulled anything strong, eg poison gas, in which event Churchill would tear up the Geneva Convention, send a bulletproof Humber tearing round to Osidge Primary, and drop the crazy bastard into Berlin. If that ever happened, we gave Hitler fifteen minutes.

David Collingwood came in once with a German nose-cap under his pullover, and the madman hit him with a chair. He must have had his own private scale of penalties for Jerrybilia; if we'd ever caught a parachutist on the allotments (probably the greatest dream any of us ever entertained, not excluding Susan Hayward), he would doubtless have taken us down to the boiler-room and hanged us.

And here I am, you know how many years on, standing in the loft with the shrapnel in my hand. The headmaster handed all confiscated relics back at the VE-Day party, as if the German capitulation had miraculously rendered them harmless. That is why I have only one piece of shrapnel left: I swopped the rest with Gerald Finch, who was sitting next to me, in return for his signed letter from the King, thanking all children for helping him win the war.

I am currently holding that in my other hand. Forty years on I still feel uneasy about it. I feel uneasy about it because, although there is no name on it to blow the gaff to posterity, it is not my letter. This is Gerald Finch's letter. As a matter of fact, I am curiously relieved to get that off my chest; it has been something of a burden, all these years.

It is not that, four long decades ago, I received no gratitude from HM George VI. It was there, beside the gift mug with the transfer on it, when I sat down at the trestle table in the playground. I read it, and I looked at the signature, and Dorothy Pickering opposite said I bet he didn't sign every one, I bet that's not real ink, and I licked my finger and rubbed the signature, and it wasn't real, and Dorothy Pickering said You should've washed, it's got a big dirty smear on it now, you can't frame that, so I got my handkerchief out and tried to rub the dirt off and the print started coming away, and Gerald Finch said Now you've done it, I bet you can go to prison for mucking up a king's letter.

Then he offered to let me have his, in return for my shrapnel collection. I wonder what happened to Gerald Finch? Probably a multi-millionaire, by now.

So all I have left is this one piece, and when I touch it, it is as with Proust sinking a delicate incisor into his madeleine: *The Night The Fairey Aviation Works at Hayes Got It* leaps from the pop-up book of infant memory with all its sense-data intact.

I can hear the greenhouse at 4 Copland Avenue collapse. I can smell the dust from the carpet inside the Morrison shelter in the dining room being beaten into my nostrils by the concussions a mile away. I can see the lurching shadows on the dining-room wall projected by the orange glow flaring up when my grandfather tore open the blackout curtains to see what the crash was all about, and hear him shouting, 'They've got the greenhouse! They've got the greenhouse!', as if it had been the Luftwaffe's main priority, Dornier pilots five miles up cheering and congratulating one another on having at last wiped out the tomatoes at 4 Copland Avenue, breaking radio silence to inform an ecstatic Goering, leaning out into the chill blackness to paint another greenhouse on the fuselage, turning joyously for home, arms linked, singing.

And this is the piece of shrapnel that did it.

I went out in the morning with my grandfather, who had painted DAVE on the tin helmet he always wore outdoors in case he was buried by rubble and rendered indistinguishable, and I picked up the piece of shrapnel, and, a lifetime on, I can still recall not only that it felt warm, but exactly *how* warm.

Halt! Who goes there?

SCHOOL IN GLASGOW

KATHARINE WHITEHORN

Painting the scenery

MY MOTHER WAS married to an English schoolmaster, so she grudgingly let my first three schools be English ones. But when I ran away from the last one, a prison named Roedean, she suggested what she had probably known all along was best: a day school in Glasgow.

After a good deal of arrangement, she managed to find somewhere for me to stay in a family, since my father's school was down south; and I presented myself on the first day in the vast, stone-floored echoing premises of the Glasgow High School for Girls. On the Wednesday I entered the third form. There was stationery to be bought (a novelty for a boarding-school child), a tram to come and go on (weird for a Londoner) and it all seemed as alarming as any other new school – well, I was familiar enough with that one.

On Friday something happened which I could scarcely believe. A couple of pleasant girls – I can't now remember whether it was Sheila or Marjorie or Elma – came up and said that as I was new and didn't know anybody, would I like to come to tea with them tomorrow to meet the girls?

A *new girl*, invited to tea! And *because* she was new! Nothing like that would ever have happened at Roedean. There, you were kept thoroughly in your place; sneered at if not actually teased; kept out; given a proper sense of your own insignificance. Only if you made the grade (and I never did) were you slowly and reluctantly admitted to human society in your second term. Yet here were these friendly Scots girls going out of their way to welcome me.

I only dimly recall the actual tea party. And I wouldn't say that never a harsh word passed between any of the Scots girls and me, ever. There was one heated argument about whether Roman Catholic ideas could ever be, as the English teacher had off-handedly said, 'quite practical'; when I supported her, a Minister's daughter from the seat behind hissed 'You're a wee Nun!' But from that moment on, I realised it was actually possible to be both happy and at school: a revelation.

Life On The Estate

GERALD GROSVENOR,
DUKE OF WESTMINSTER

ITHINK I HAD what can only be called the most blissful childhood possible. I was brought up on Lough Erne, outside Enniskillen in Northern Ireland, and it was my home for the first nineteen years of my life – until my uncle, the fourth duke, died. The lake was fifty-two miles long with 365 islands on it, and our home was on one of them – about 170 acres. It was like *Swallows and Amazons*. We had all the danger and excitement of living on water and mucking about in boats – spending hours on the lough and coming back wet and filthy, or fishing from the minutest little boats. How we didn't drown ourselves I don't know!

There were five of us: my two sisters and our two boy cousins who lived with us. My parents were great ones for freedom in every sense, and really we were allowed a horrifying amount. It was the kind of freedom which, sadly, isn't possible today. We'd amble along those island shores with heavy deposits of blue clay which one could easily get stuck in. Or we'd be up in the hills at two in the morning, hunting. Being an old wartime base, the island was covered in unexploded bombs and things.

We had a lot of animals around – farm animals, sheep, donkeys, ponies. I spent a lot of time with the eel fishermen and also the boat-builders on the lough, who used to build Erne barges. The farmers used to move their cattle in these barges across from the mainland to graze on the islands. Sometimes they swam the cattle across and I helped them. I did a lot of swimming. I also fished, and sometimes I water-skied. It was wonderful.

I was doubly lucky because there was nothing attached to my name when I was young: I was just plain Gerald Grosvenor. As a child, I really didn't know I was coming into all this. In fact, we were kept on a tight financial rein. I once asked my father if we could have a rowing boat and he said 'No', which rather dismayed me. So we built a raft out of drums, which promptly sank. We had a miniscule amount of pocket money but we supplemented it by hunting foxes. We didn't hunt for sport, it was more to control the vermin. There was a good bounty on foxes – £1 for a vixen and ten shillings for a dog fox.

As the nearest town was about eight miles away, we were isolated, and so our influences came from within the family. In the early years, my mother was a tremendous influence. My father was more of an influence in later years, because his work – he was MP for Fermanagh & South Tyrone – took him away from home a lot. He and I were very close. When he died, someone said to me: 'You've not only lost a father but a partner as well.'

IN THE COALHOUSE

BARBARA CASTLE

A budding politician

I WAS BROUGHT UP in a literary family. Of course, it was a Socialist family so my parents believed in exploring all the great ideas and writings in the world. Even when we children were very young we used to take part in family 'reading' by the fireside every Sunday evening, when my father would introduce us to the works of Homer and William Morris and other masterpieces which we did not always understand, but whose literary aura we drank in.

Later we used to listen in to readings by adult gatherings in our home of Bernard Shaw, Shakespeare, H.G. Wells. It was often above our heads, but we grew up in the belief that reading and dramatic performances were an essential part of life.

We were lucky in my mother. Although my father, a brilliant intellectual whom she adored, dominated the household, it was she who always saw to it that we children were not overpowered by him. Money was always short, partly because my father insisted on living in a house big enough for him to have his own study, where he could retire away from us all to his beloved books. So we children never had the little luxuries most middle-class children had. I never owned a tennis racket, or a bicycle, had holidays abroad or wore smart clothes, but in other ways we had opportunities for self-expression which other children lacked. My mother saw to that.

I was about ten when we first went to live in a roomy house in Toller Lane, Bradford. My father had his study and mother decided we children should each have our own hideaway, too. Eventually we were all satisfied. My brother chose a cellar for his den, which she painted a vivid red at his request, and decorated it with a large skull and crossbones in black. My elder sister had a reasonably normal attic room

and there was only the outside coalhouse left for me. Nothing daunted my mother scrubbed it out, painted the walls white, put in a couple of chairs and a little table. I can't remember where she put the coal. It was narrow, but tall enough for our purposes. It was here that I mobilised my little gang of schoolfriends into a literary club of grandiose pretensions.

The coalhouse had one drawback: it had no window. If we were not to sit in the dark and stifle, we had to keep the door open during all our gatherings. The door opened on to a small backyard. On one side we were sheltered by the garage, which was used as a storehouse because we had no car. On the other side a wall divided us from our neighbour's yard. On wet days we would crowd into our narrow room. On fine days we would spill out into the yard.

I had all sorts of ideas for our activities. We must, I declared, produce a newspaper, full of school gossip, pen portraits and political articles. I was unanimously elected editor and I soon realised why. No editor ever had a team of contributors more reluctant to put pen to paper, and I ended by writing most of the articles myself.

Tired of this one-sided activity I suggested that we should produce a play. What about *Julius Caesar*, which we were just beginning to read at school? The steps leading up to our back door would make an excellent stage. Once again my gang concurred obligingly, but once again they were slow to learn their parts. To encourage them I sprang on to the steps and launched into Mark Antony's speech. 'Friends, Romans, countrymen,' I declaimed dramatically, when I heard a giggle from behind our neighbour's wall. Looking over I saw our neighbour's fourteen-year-old son crouching down out of sight and enjoying himself enormously at our expense.

The horrible truth dawned on me. The beastly boy must have been listening-in on us for months. He could have heard all our schoolgirl confidences, the reading aloud of our newspapers and other literary activities through the coalhouse's open door. I stormed at him in fury and, still giggling, he slipped away. But our secrecy had been dealt a mortal blow. 'Julius Caesar' came to an abrupt end. The newspaper was wound up. The literary club lost its attractiveness. Gradually the coalhouse reverted to its normal use.

GOODBYE BUDGIE

ERNIE WISE

I REMEMBER AS A little boy of nine years of age appearing in the working men's clubs in Leeds and Bradford. I was doing a double act with my father called Carson and Kid.

At one particular club I recall, I danced on the billiard table and during the course of the evening the organisers had a raffle and the prize was a budgerigar in a cage, which I would have loved to have taken home with me because I have always loved animals. Needless to say, I didn't win the budgerigar, but seeing my disappointment I was promised one for the following year when I returned to the club.

So all the next year I looked forward, with great anticipation, to my budgerigar in a cage. The great day arrived. I went back to the club and danced on the billiard table. They didn't forget and I was duly presented with a budgerigar. I was overjoyed. I took it home that night and hung it in my bedroom.

The following morning I woke up and there was my bird. However, as I don't like to see birds in cages, I released the budgerigar and let it fly about my bedroom. I then went to the bathroom to brush my teeth.

My mother meanwhile came into my bedroom to make the bed. She opened the window to let some fresh air into the room . . .

Goodbye budgie.

Playing the clubs

TAKING THE PLUNGE

MAVIS NICHOLSON

THERE WAS A time when religion filled my life.

Sunday school in our Baptist chapel at the age of four was loving and gentle. You sat on nursery chairs in a small semicircle round your teacher. She had on her best clothes and smelt flowery from the scent dabbed on the handkerchief tucked up her sleeve. This she would lend you if you suddenly sneezed.

She taught you things you could easily understand and, in particular, that Jesus loved the very young. There he was on the wall behind the piano, his arm held out over the lambs which surrounded him, and saying, 'Suffer Little Children to Come Unto Me'.

In that traily little way of four-year-olds, helped by our teacher's fruity voice, we all used to sing:

> *Jesus bids us shine*
> *With a pure, clear light*
> *Like a little candle*
> *Burning in the night*
>
> *In this world of darkness*
> *We-ee must shine*
> *You in your small corner*
> *And I in mine*

Such language used to make me immensely happy as a young child.

By the time I was fourteen I was almost convinced that God had chosen me. Here I was, this energetic tomboy, full of cheek and only too ready to say what I felt. Surely sensitive, too, for wasn't I being continually moved to tears by hymn-singing or the organ playing Handel's Largo or by Beethoven's Moonlight Sonata? So wasn't I just the sort of humble person who ought to become a missionary?

It was inevitable, then, that I should choose to be baptised around this age. There were about eight of us who had decided to take the plunge (which we literally did as Baptists). We met for the preparatory talks with the minister in his chintzy, book-lined study. Not a word of them do I remember now. But in essence I agreed with everything. Believing in God's word . . . Yes. Feeling chosen to spread His message . . . Yes, yes. Serving Him in every way that I could . . . Yes, yes, yes, yes.

We were told the meaning of our baptism, our total immersion. We were like

Christ. We would die as we descended into the pool. We would be buried, symbolically, as the water went over our body and head. Then we would rise again, and like Christ be resurrected. We would be purified and cleansed of all our sins.

On the chosen Sunday morning we sat through the service, which was a bit shorter than usual, waiting for our turn to come. Below the altar, the pool, which was normally covered over, now lay glinting, greeny-blue.

While the boys wore white shirts and trousers, we were in tennis dresses. An elastic band around the hem of the skirt so that it wouldn't ride up in the water. No shoes, just white socks.

Our minister, in thigh-high waders and black flowing robes, waited solemnly in the pool for us to enter, shyly, one by one.

It was icy. As the water came up to my waist I could hear myself making great gulping noises (I have always been scared, anyway, of ducking my head below the water). But as I came out again, when a deacon at the edge of the pool threw a cloak around me, and the congregation sang, 'Hosanna, Hosanna, Hosanna', I must say it was a moment of wonderful exaltation.

ACROSS THE TRANSPORTER BRIDGE

LESLIE THOMAS

STORIES RUN IN our family. My father, a wandering Welsh sailor, would come in with the tide, overflowing with yarns of ships and places, although as far as the places were concerned he often wrongly pronounced them and his knowledge of where they were located was not considerable. 'Well,' he answered when once someone remarked on this. 'It's being a stoker, see. I'm hardly on the deck from the time we sail to the time we tie up. How do *I* know where the ports are? All I know is I've *been* there.'

Similarly my mother responded to drama. Romance, tragedy, weepy songs, stirring hymns, disasters of the larger variety, weddings and especially funerals ('Oh well, it was a nice day out wasn't it?') were the enjoyments of her life, to be retold often and with increasing exaggeration. Even my birth was a tall story. According to

her it took place in the pricey privacy of a nursing home on Stow Hill, the highest point of Newport, Monmouthshire. This was an elevation in more ways than one because thereafter there were times when we could scarcely manage the cost of a bed, let alone a nursing home. 'There was a terrible thunder storm,' my mother would relate, eyes beginning to glow, hands beginning to move. She had a throaty Barry Island voice. 'Terrible. Bangs and electric shocks all round the bed.' Another, possibly pregnant, wait. 'And there was me, sitting up, see . . . singing!' I could believe that. She had a faltering Welsh wail. She claimed she had sung 'Rock of Ages' between thunder claps.

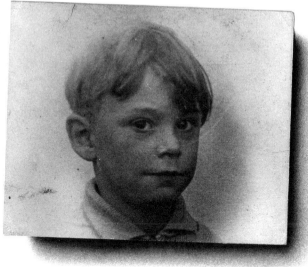

Leslie Thomas, aged 5

My parents agreed on little but they would gladly call an armistice to verify each other's tall stories. Like the one about the dog we had who one night came home, pleased enough, with a whole quiver of bones from the St Woolos burial ground. The road was being widened and he had taken advantage of the excavations to do some digging on his own account. In this story they actually *lived* ('in residence' according to my mother) on Stow Hill, possibly to be near the nursing home, but the first domicile of my memory was two rooms in Milner Street down by the murky and mucky River Usk, not far from the Transporter Bridge.

Now there *was* a wonder, the Transporter Bridge. We were told at school that it was one of only two in the country and a Frenchman was brought over specially to build it. I do not doubt that. It must have been the most uneconomic way of ever taking goods, people and vehicles from one side of a river to the other. In recent years the town discovered that it would cost more to demolish it than to keep it; so they kept it. It has two massive steel structures, one on each bank, like the towers you see above Texas oil wells but taller. Between the towers is a meccano-set bridge and slung below this on cables, a platform pulled by hawsers from one side of the river to the other. For a boy it used to cost a penny to go across.

It was a child's delight to make that journey from bank to muddy bank of the Usk. I used to pretend I was going to another country. It was like travelling in the gondola of an airship, whirring slowly through space, the broad, black-tongued river curling below, little ships lying like dogs against its bank. On one side you could see the other more conventional town bridge and its traffic, the green cupola of the Technical College, with the wharves and warehouses and the stump of the ancient

castle. Electric trams travelled in the distance, making sparks on dark days. On the other side of the Transporter, beyond the puffing steelworks, the river yawned to the Bristol Channel. Misty miles away it seemed, the gateway, as my father pointed out to me in a scene reminiscent of the Boyhood of Raleigh, to the wide and amazing world. To look directly down below from the moving platform was to experience a delicious terror; snakes of thick water wriggled between slime coated by coal-dust drifting from the Welsh valleys. It was legend that people had fallen or jumped and been sucked up by the hungry mud. I used to imagine them lying down deep, engulfed by the stuff . . . *preserved*. When the tide was up the river flowed strongly, but still foul and thick as if its bed were on top. One day, however, we saw a blithe sailing boat with scarlet sails on the moribund water and my mother burst into a loud and embarrassing chorus of a song called 'Red Sails In The Sunset'. I had to ask her to stop and I could have only been four years old.

On another day she made a gallop for the travelling platform moments before its gate slammed, almost dragging me off the ground in her hurry. An avid funeral-spotter she had seen that the bridge's cargo was nothing less than a cortège, the hearse and the two mourners' cars standing dreadly beside a horse and cart and various pedestrians looking decently the other way. No such embarrassment discouraged my Mam. We stood holding hands, neither of us being able to take our eyes from the glistening wood and shining handles of the coffin as the platform began its crossing. Unable to restrain herself any longer Mam approached the first mourning car and tapped politely but firmly on the closed window. A distraught and astonished face was framed when the glass had been lowered. 'Who is it?' she inquired in a huge whisper jerking her head towards the hearse. The wind was blowing down the Usk and the platform was swaying.

Hardly able to credit the inquiry the mourner, a man in a black bowler hat, haltingly told her the identity of the deceased. My Mam thanked him and whispered: 'There's a pity,' before the window was hurriedly rolled up again. Only a toddler, I witnessed this brazenness with amazement and admiration. She returned to me and once more took hold of my hand. 'Nobody we know,' she confided.

Along the river bank from the Transporter Bridge was a wharf beside the steelworks. One morning in the unemployed nineteen-thirties, my father took me there to act as bait in getting a job aboard a little coaster. 'Suck your cheeks in. Try to look half-starved,' he suggested as we went aboard. It was not difficult. I had seen my mother burst into tears when, having seen the plates put out for tea I inquired: 'Well, there's the plates – all we want now is something to put on them.'

The skipper of the coaster was presumably impressed by the waif because he not only gave my father the job as a stoker on his weekly-boat (so named because it went to Ireland and back in a week) but took us to his cabin where he spread out a hundred or more coins on his polished table. It was like a treasure and my eyes shone. 'Let's see what we can give the boy,' ruminated the captain. He shuffled the

wealth about while I trembled with anticipation but eventually decided that every coin was foreign except one, a halfpenny, which he pressed with ceremony into my hand.

During his workless times, and they lasted weeks and months, my father used to look disconsolately for odd jobs ashore, sit at home eating bread and cheese (all he ever ate) or go to the public library to stare at the papers. When he got his dole money my mother would escort him to make sure he did not head for the nearest public bar. Once, the money in his pocket, he abruptly announced that he had been informed in a vision that our house was on fire. Before she could stop him (I was with them and she was holding my hand and that of my young brother) he had loped off into the dusk. He came home at midnight, plastered and penniless, and she threw the chamber pot over his head. Hurt and in a huff he went away and we did not see him again for nearly two years. Then he turned up in the middle of the night. He had been on a ship to Argentina and was dressed in a gaucho's outfit and plucking a guitar. He said he thought it would make her laugh.

There was an announcement one day that a free concert was to be given for the children of the unemployed. It was held at an extraordinary Grecian building with white portico and marble columns, which sat incongruously amid the straight streets and was the steelworks social institute. My father took me and I sat enthralled by the various acts that attempted to temporarily alleviate the misery of the workless. We sang with feeling a song called 'I Do Like Potatoes And Gravy', a social commentary if ever there was one. One performance thrilled me more than any, a whistler who whistled through his fingers while adopting various poses, on a bicycle, on a chair, and standing on his head. It seemed to me that he whistled better when he was upside down than he did when the right way up. When he had finished the applause shook the Grecian columns. 'Oh Dad,' I enthused. 'He was good, wasn't he!'

His reply was heartfelt: 'There's too many of them,' he said.

from *In My Wildest Dreams*

OUT OF THE MOUTHS OF BABES AND SUCKLINGS

JOHN EBDON

FAIR-HAIRED AND blue-eyed with features like that of a Botticelli angel, the girl-child gazed at my face with unwavering concentration, mutely listening as my friend and I recalled memories of boyhood days long past. How gratifying, I thought as I watched her from the corner of my eye, that our nostalgic ramblings should enthrall her so completely. There was, I pondered, much good in the modern child despite widely held opinions to the contrary, and privately I congratulated myself on my success as a spellbinder. For a long, long while she eyed me in silence, her head cradled in her hands. Then, as I arrested my narration to light my pipe, she spoke.

'Excuse me,' she said with exquisite politeness and an engaging lisp, 'but did you know you've a hair growing out of the top of your ear?'

Disbelievingly and with a dented ego I stared glassily at her through the smoke and allowed the match to peter out. 'No,' I said, 'I didn't. Where?' 'There!' said she, and pointed toward the target area. Slowly I guided my fingers toward the member under discussion. 'Um,' she said, her eyes brightening with encouragement as I found the exhibit, 'that's it – the long black crinkly one.' She paused. 'That means you're getting old, doesn't it?' I nodded bleakly, my self esteem continuing to evaporate. 'Yes,' I said, 'I suppose it does'; and swallowed hard. There was another pause. Then, without malice but delicately placing a verbal rapier between my third and fourth ribs, she administered the *coup de grâce*. 'Tell me,' she asked, 'what's it feel like to be old? *Really* old I mean?' I was forty-six at the time . . .

Happily we are still good friends and since that day, and with her own eight-year-old daughter in attendance, I have taken my revenge by reminding her of that conversation. However, on reflection the *mauvais quart d'heure* which she then afforded me was no more than poetic justice: in Switzerland at the age of six I too had caused hurt and havoc among my elders by my lack of inhibition and frankness.

'But *why*,' shrilled a formidable and totally resistible Swiss woman dressed in black bombasine and who, with a hirsute upper lip moved in an aura of stale mothballs, 'will you not kiss me, *mon petit chou*?' 'Because,' said her petit chou, fiercely repulsing her attempts to embrace him and displacing her pince-nez the while, 'your moustache pricks me, and you smell of old clothes.'

It was an unhappy moment in our family history and particularly for my nanny

The boy Ebdon

who was privy to my enormity. Unfairly, in my opinion, those in authority adjudged her guilty by default of playing a major part in the event which led to the severing of diplomatic relations between my mother and the outraged Madam Fournier. She should, it was argued, have prevented me from giving tongue; and, if necessary, by force. Nonetheless, she remained in my mother's employ and I became indebted to her: Nanny Françoise introduced me to astronomy.

Although clearly not a product of the Norland Stables – indeed she originated from a village in the Jura – she was a lovable, deeply religious and surprisingly erudite person possessed of three consuming interests: gin; the stars; and myself; and in that order of priority. Consequently, nearly every star she saw was a binary, and most of the planets and constellations which swam into her ken were blurred at the edges; but it was through her that my appetite for the subject was whetted. It was she who guided my eyes to beyond the frosted roofs of La Chaux-de-fonds and into the dark Swiss skies where swung the Great and Little Bears around the stationary Pole Star; and it was she who showed me the fire-fly beauty of the Pleiades and the majesty of Orion the Hunter. 'Ah,' she would whisper, her arm around my shoulders, 'are they not wonderful, *mon petit homme*, those tiny stars? And was it not clever of *Le Bon Dieu* to put them there?'

Nearly sixty years have passed since those innocent childhood days and Nanny Françoise has long since departed from this planet. But on winter nights when the frost is keen and the stars shine out like diamonds, her ghost stands by me in the darkness looking upward, and once again I hear her voice: 'Are they not wonderful, those tiny stars?' And I think of the words of Emerson which unknowingly she echoed:

'If the stars should appear one night in a thousand years, how would men believe and adore; and preserve for many generations the City of God which had been shown!'